P9-DHP-836

THE FIRST

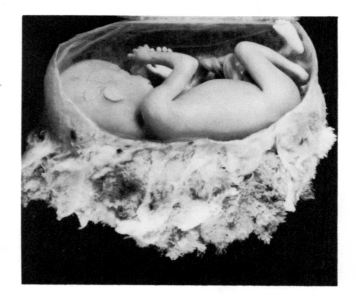

NINE MONTHS
OF LIFE

by Geraldine Lux Flanagan

SIMON AND SCHUSTER · NEW YORK

ISBN 0-671-26105-3
LIBRARY OF CONGRESS CATALOG CARD NUMBER 62-9605
MANUFACTURED IN THE UNITED STATES OF AMERICA

11   12   13   14   15   16   17   18   19   20

The First Nine Months of Life is also issued in the following
languages by the indicated publishers:
DANISH : Steen Hasselbalchs Forlag, Copenhagen, Denmark
DUTCH : "Contact" Uitgeverij, Amsterdam, The Netherlands
FINNISH : Werner Söderström, Helsinki, Finland
FRENCH : Editions Robert Laffont, Paris, France
GERMAN : Rowohlt Verlag, Reinbek bei Hamburg, Germany
HEBREW : Sadan Publishing House Ltd., Tel-Aviv, Israel
ITALIAN : Casa Editrice Valentino Bompiani, Milan, Italy
JAPANESE : Mirai-Sha Ltd., Tokyo, Japan
NORWEGIAN : J. W. Cappelens Forlag, Oslo, Norway
POLISH : Panstwowy Zaklad Wydawnictw Lekarskich,
        Warsaw, Poland
PORTUGUESE : Publicaçoès Europa-America, Lisbon, Portugal
SPANISH : Editorial Seix Barral, Barcelona, Spain
SWEDISH : Bokforlaget Forum, Stockholm, Sweden
The BRITISH edition is published by William Heinemann Ltd.,
London, England

TO CARA AND JOHN

For there is no king had any other first beginning.
For all men have one entrance into life...
　　　The Wisdom of Solomon *in the Apocrypha*

CONTENTS

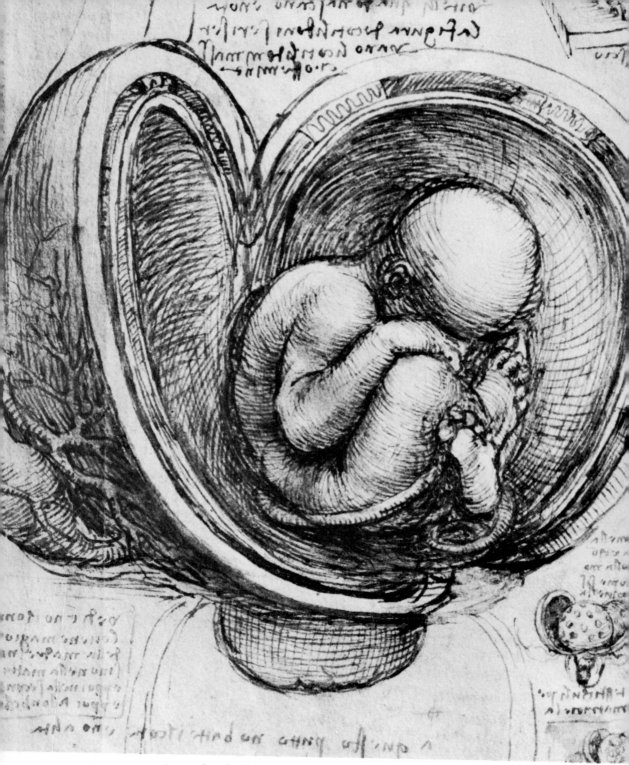

LEONARDO DA VINCI sketched the unborn infant in his notebooks of 1510–12. "Do you see how the great vessels of the mother pass into the uterus," he wrote in his customary left-handed mirror writing. The bottom line, "*A questo putto* [baby] *non batto il core*," indicates that he wrongly believed this infant had no need of a beating heart because it was "vivified and nourished by the life of the mother." [Royal Collection, Windsor Castle, copyright reserved.]

PREFACE

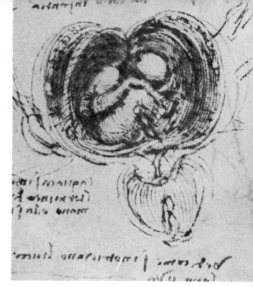

WE ARE THE FIRST GENERATION to be able to have a clear picture of the course of our development from a single cell to an individual, active and responsive to our environment long before birth. We are also the first to know the full history of our earliest hours and days. The ripened human egg cell coming from the ovary was first seen in 1930. The union of the human parent cells, sperm and egg, was not observed until fourteen years later, in 1944. The events of our initial six days of life became known in the 1950s. Now in the 1960s we are finally beginning to decipher the intricate cell structures that shape our heredity.

"All seeds have the umbilical cord which breaks when the seed is mature....Those which grow in nutshells as hazelnuts...have the umbilical cord long which shows itself in their infancy," wrote Leonardo, who believed that "man is part... of one great unity of all living beings."

The science of embryology is a comparatively young one. The minute egg cell of mammals (all animals that produce milk; from the Latin *mamma,* meaning breast) was not identified until the nineteenth century. It was found in 1827 by the Estonian biologist Karl Ernst von Baer, when he examined the ovary of a dog under the microscope. The microscope had been perfected a hundred and fifty years earlier, but Von Baer was the first to recognize what had escaped others before him. As he wrote in his treatise, *De Ovi Mammalium et Hominis Genesi:*

I saw plainly ... a yellowish-white point ... led by

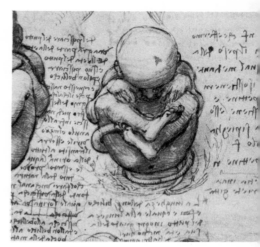

"*Del pisciare del putto*" begins the description on this sketch that mistakenly assumes the infant to be immobile, with one heel shutting off urine before birth.

curiosity . . . I opened one of the follicles and took up the minute object on the point of my knife, finding that I could see it very distinctly. When I placed it under the microscope I was utterly astonished for I saw an ovule [an immature egg cell] and so clearly that a blind man could hardly deny it.

While the science of embryology is a recent one, man's interest and curiosity in the subject are old. Aristotle observed the development of a chick embryo more than two thousand years ago. Without the microscope, he could not see the very small structures of the initial stages of development. From what he could see of the chick, he inferred that the human embryo develops out of an ''admixture of the male seminal fluid and the menstrual blood.'' The direction of his thinking was correct but he made one error. He thought the substance of the embryo came solely from the female while the male provided only the stimulus for growth. Five hundred years later, in the second century A.D., the Greek physician, Galen, gave an added interpretation, an essentially incorrect one, that persisted for more than fifteen hundred years. Galen proposed a theory that later became known as *emboîtement,* meaning incasement or encapsulation. It came to be thought that minute prefabricated embryos existed in the ''female semen,'' and that contact with the male merely brought about an unshelling of such an embryo, permitting it to increase in size until birth. Every baby must therefore contain a preformed baby, one stacked inside the other like Chinese boxes.

In a sense, Galen and those who later taught

the concept of preformation were not entirely wrong. Theirs was a good guess, expressed in oversimplified terms. We know today that the body of a baby is not so literally contained in preformed fashion within the mother. It is a more subtle dowry of heritage that is passed on from parent to child. The dowry is inscribed in the genes of the reproductive cells and the material of these, passed on from one generation to the next, is held in trust in our bodies. Indeed, symbolically like Chinese boxes, the genetic material does incorporate the heritage of our species and will mold its future.

Near the end of the seventeenth century, the microscope was perfected. In 1677 the Dutch naturalist, Anton van Leeuwenhoek, could see for the first time a living male reproductive cell, the sperm, in a drop of seminal fluid. By this time another Dutchman, a young physi-

A fifteenth-century illustration of a child in the womb is typically stylized and reflects the medieval resistance to biological realism.

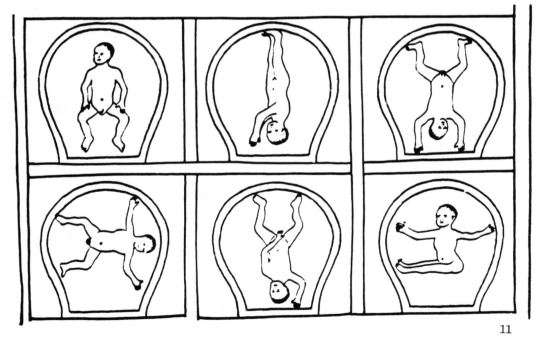

11

cian, Regnier de Graaf, had seen and described something that "broke like bubbles" when he opened the reproductive tubes of a female rabbit. These were the early clusters of cells that form an embryo. But neither De Graaf nor Leeuwenhoek really understood what they had seen. They still could not imagine that a living creature is assembled from single cells, form built out of formlessness. Instead, Leeuwenhoek's finding of the sperm led to a new confusion and a scientific controversy.

In the seventeenth and eighteenth centuries, two camps of biologists grew up, one called the ovists and the other the homunculists. Both believed in *emboîtement*. But the ovists persevered in the old belief that the prefabricated baby is contained somehow in the mother's ovaries. Man's descent, they said, is matrilineal; the sperm merely serves to incite the expansion of the mother's ready-made baby. The homunculists said, no! Man is preformed in the head of the sperm. They drew pictures to illustrate their view, showing a tiny homunculus sitting with head bowed and legs crossed, neatly incased in the head of the sperm. This homunculus, they reasoned, found a fertile ground in the womb and grew there as in an incubator.

Ovists and homunculists pursued an intense dispute for nearly a hundred years until the anatomist Kaspar Friedrich Wolff trained his microscope on the embryo of the chick and, in the thesis for his medical degree at Halle University, published under the title *Theoria Generationis* in 1759, effectively demolished *emboîtement,* and ovists and homunculists. In their place he established two new and correct concepts. First, that a body is not preformed but is assembled out of "globules" and, secondly, that both parents equally contribute something to the substance of the offspring. He surmised this, although the mammal's egg cell had still not been seen. More than fifty years later, and Von Baer came to find it on the tip of his laboratory knife.

After this, in the second half of the nineteenth century, the quest for knowledge in embryology gained new vigor. The full meaning of the reproductive cells became clear after Matthias Schleiden, German botanist, and Theodor Schwann, German physiologist, discovered that all living form is built out of a basic structural unit of life, the cell (from the Latin *cella*, meaning small room). Soon thereafter the mammal's egg and sperm were identified as true cells. Now it was possible to understand how a body could be built, step by step, out of growing cells.

As the details of structure were becoming understood, a new element was introduced that caused great controversy and misunderstanding and has led many people to this day to confuse early simplicity of structure with alleged animal crudeness. This new element was the Theory of Evolution. On November 24, 1859, *On the Origin of Species* by Charles Darwin was published and all 1,250 copies of the first edition sold out in one day. Twelve years later, Darwin published *The Descent of Man,* of which he wrote in his Introduction:

During many years I collected notes on the origin or descent of man, without any intention of publish-

A homunculus drawn in 1694 by Niklaas Hartsoeker, Dutch scientist. A human with a baby's "soft spot" on his head sits inside the microscopic sperm cell.

ing on the subject, but rather with the determination not to publish, as I thought that I should thus only add to the prejudices against my views . . . . that man must be included with other organic beings in any general conclusion respecting his manner of appearance on this earth.

What was to Darwin harmonious unity in nature did not look the same to all men. The embryonic similarity between man and his fellow creatures was misunderstood by opponents of Darwin. At the same time it was exaggerated by those who supported him. The evolutionists even claimed for man an early

Prejudice against Darwin's Theory evoked a cartoon of the author and a dandy descending from worm and ape.

tail and gills—an essentially incorrect view, as we shall see in "The First Month."

Soon, at about the turn of the century, some biologists began to consider also the evolution of the behavior of an organism. After 1900, George E. Coghill began the first systematic observation of embryonic behavior. For this he chose the amphibian, Amblystoma, a salamander. In the first three decades of the twentieth century, Coghill published sixty-five scientific papers and one book, laying the foundations for our gaining an understanding of human reflex and voluntary motion.

The knowledge of the past has been as an overture to what we have learned in the most recent ten and twenty years. It gives the theme (all life from a single cell—formlessness into form, and then function in orderly sequence) but leaves the subtle details still to be discovered.

The prize for man in the study of embryology is not merely to satisfy curiosity. The knowledge of the biologist can enrich the skill of the physician. This is the frontier of embryology today: to understand the mechanism that governs and controls orderly growth in time perhaps to prevent, perhaps to treat, the puzzling departures from the orderly patterns.

The prize is also that we can try to be as intelligent about "intra-uterine" mothering as we try to be today about the care of our children after they are born. This increased awareness can also bear the fruit of increased enjoyment.

G.L.F.

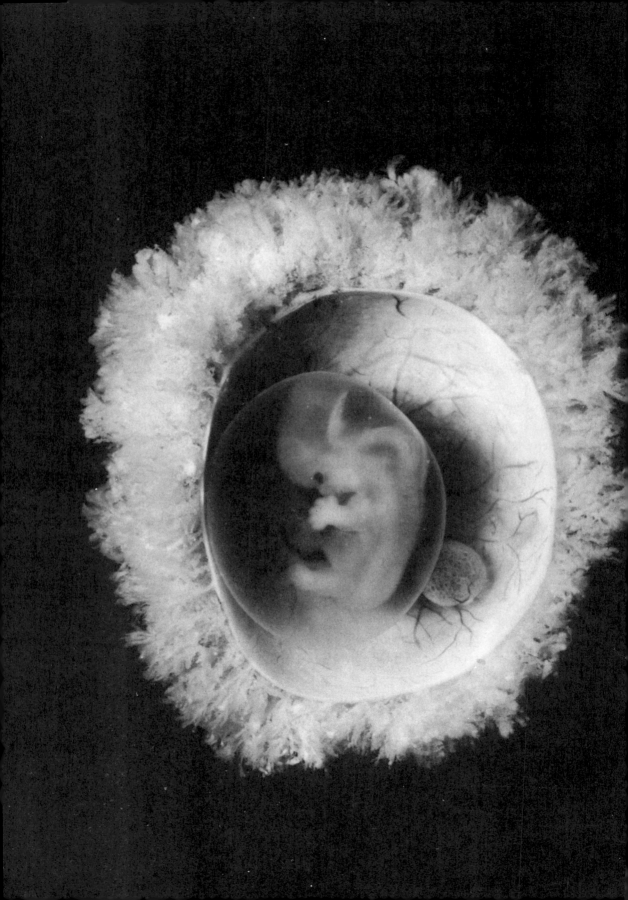

PORTRAIT AT FORTY DAYS

F<small>ORTY DAYS</small> *after mother and father have come together to create a child, the child will look just like the embryo baby in this photograph. Barely six weeks after its first beginning, the embryo has a well formed body. It is very much alive and can even execute some movements with its arms. It has a heart that has been beating for two weeks. It has a brain and nervous system sending out impulses. It has the outlines of a complete though still soft skeleton and all the vital organs, some of them practicing their functions. On close examination it is already possible to know whether this embryo is a boy or girl.*

The forty-day-old human is so small it would fit into a walnut. It weighs less than a book of paper matches. The forty-day-old embryo is still a long way from being able to live without an intimate life line to the mother. For all its apparent perfection, it is still far from completing its development. It has fulfilled only one-sixth (forty of the 266 days) of the normal stay in the womb.

The pages that follow give us a kind of window into the womb. Through it we can watch a baby from his first moment, his real birth, which precedes the day of being born by nine months.

Photograph of a forty-day-old human embryo surrounded by the tissues that protect and root it in the womb.

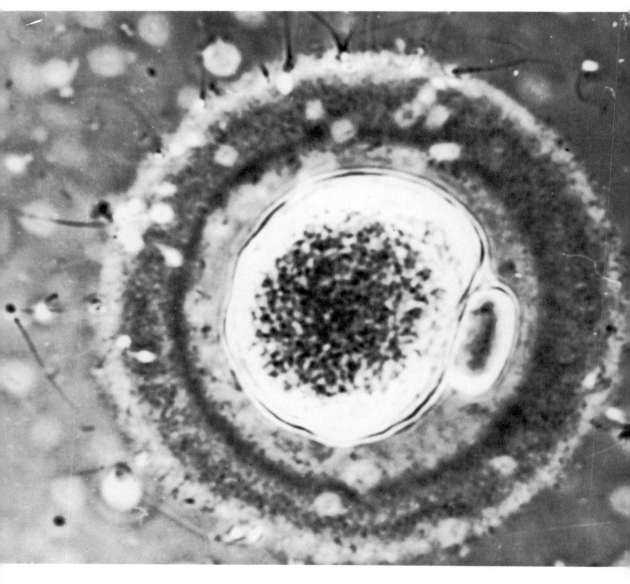

THE FIRST DAY

Before I was born out of my mother generations
guided me . . .

Walt Whitman

A BABY BEGINS LIFE as a single cell, smaller than the period at the end of this sentence, and would be only barely visible to the naked eye. This cell is created by the union of two parent cells: the female egg cell or ovum, and the male sperm cell.

The parent cells have a twofold function in reproduction. Together they initiate the most remarkable and dynamic event in nature: the assembly of a living body out of single molecules of proteins, carbohydrates and other biochemicals. In addition, the parent cells control the specific design of the baby. It is a design that will follow a pattern passed along a chain of inheritance, going back to the biological

Human parent cells (magnified 1,000 diameters) commence union which may be completed in thirty-five hours. Here tadpole-like sperm cells approach the egg and attempt penetration.

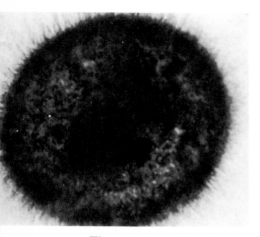

The exterior of the human egg covered by sperm cells, whose thread-fine tails stand out, beating to propel the sperms ahead.

The translucent shell of the human egg, here removed, is a tough but pliable elastic membrane.

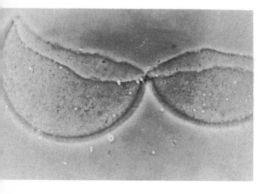

roots of this family. In a sense, each new life actually has no definite beginning. Its existence is inherent in the existence of the parent cells and these, in turn, have arisen from the preceding parent cells. When any two parent cells unite, they bring together a blend of the attributes of all ancestors before them. Thus, since all people are descended from a small number of early human beings, they are all linked by a common heritage.

In the photograph on page 18 we see the event that immediately precedes the union of parent cells. Dr. Landrum B. Shettles, a research biologist and obstetrician, made this photograph through the eyepiece of a microscope. He recovered a living but unfertilized egg from one of the two female reproductive glands, the ovaries. The human egg cell is as small as the point of a very fine needle; it is light yellow, for the pin-point egg contains a fragment of yolk; and it is round as a ball. Working with jewelers' tools, Dr. Shettles placed the fragile egg in a warm, sterile salt solution in a laboratory glass dish. Then he secured some fresh sperm cells and added these to the fluid containing the egg. The male cells are far smaller than the egg. Twenty-five hundred sperm would be needed to cover a period. The sperm cells are often likened to miniature tadpoles because they have a similar appearance and can swim. Unlike the egg, the male cells have the power of locomotion. The rapid back-and-forth lashing of their tails propels the sperm cells ahead. In the fluid of the laboratory glass dish they swim about at random. But as soon as one of them reaches the egg it becomes excited; its tail lashes about more rapidly, pushing the head forward to penetrate the protective covering of the egg. This outer cover is a shimmering, transparent but tough membrane called zona pellucida, the pellucid zone.

The male cell does not penetrate the egg's cover by force alone. It is aided in its progress by a special chemical substance, a digestive enzyme, contained in the sperm. The potent enzyme helps the sperm to actually eat its way through the pellucid zone and then through a finer underlying membrane that holds the substance of the egg. When this is accomplished, the male cell has entered into the body of the

The interior of the egg is traversed by a successful sperm cell heading for the female nucleus. The egg's volume is eighty-five thousand times that of the sperm.

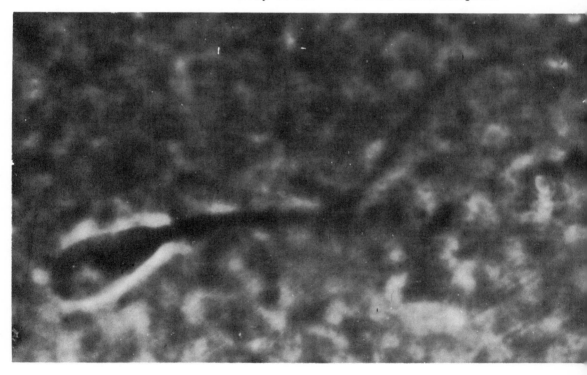

egg. But to complete union, the male cell must still forge ahead to reach the center of the egg and join with the female cell nucleus. The ensuing fusion of the two is called fertilization, and it is the vital event which initiates the development of a baby. It has been observed that more than one male cell can enter the egg, but it is thought that only the first to reach the female nucleus can complete fertilization, thereby shutting out the competing sperm cells. In the light verse of Aldous Huxley:

A million million spermatozoa,
All of them alive:
Out of their cataclysm but one poor
    Noah
Dare hope to survive.

We can observe the union of parent cells under the microscope, but we can never see or even acknowledge it when it takes place in the sheltered recesses of the mother's body. There is no physical sign that heralds the event. Therefore, we can never be sure when it occurs, but we can be reasonably certain how it must occur.

The female egg comes from the ovary of the mother. The mother has two ovaries and these contain more than a quarter million immature egg cells, some present from the time of her birth. Normally, one egg ripens each month in the alternate ovary, approximately two weeks before an expected menstruation. The ripe egg bursts out of the ovary and falls into the trumpet-shaped opening of a hollow tube. This is the ovarian, or Fallopian tube, which has an

The form of the human egg and its shell shows up under reflected light in this photomicrograph.

internal diameter the size of a hair bristle and is about four inches long. One such tube leads from each ovary to the mother's womb, the uterus. The minute round egg is slowly wafted toward the uterus by a gentle current of maternal fluids within the tube. The egg has a very brief life and would soon disintegrate to less than a grain of dust. To survive, it must be fertilized and activated by a male cell on the first or, at most, on the second day after its arrival in the tube.

The male cells are produced in the testicles of the father. It is thought that many millions of new cells are constantly being manufactured and that the cells that reach the mother are usually fresh ones. Like the female cells, the

The compact heads and strong tails of sperm cells are shown by reflected light in a microscopic drop of male seminal fluid.

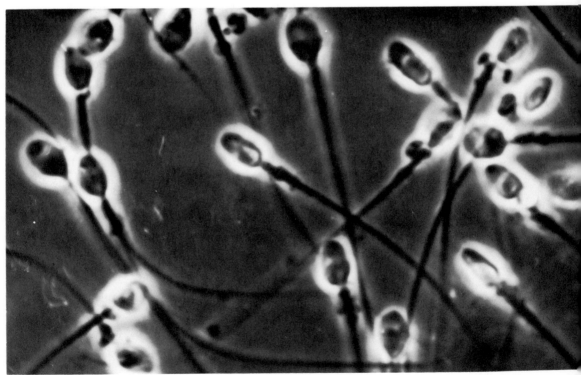

male cells have a very brief life span. They retain their fertile vigor for no more than one to two days after leaving the testicles. The short life of the sperm cells and of the egg cell limits the period during each menstrual cycle in which a baby can be conceived. The period is usually confined to two days during any one month. The chance for conception in the brief period of fertility is greatly enhanced by the fact that the father normally produces a vast excess of reproductive cells. At least twenty million and often as many as five hundred million sperm cells should be present in a single ejaculation. Nature provides an abundance of cells but many millions of them inevitably fall by the wayside after they have been introduced into the mother's body. Only a few dozen of the original millions reach the vicinity of the egg, which at this time is still drifting high up in the ovarian tube. It has been estimated that the successful male cells traverse the seven-inch distance, edging forward in hit-or-miss fashion, in a little over an hour.

Each sperm cell brings the father's contribution of inheritance to the egg. Among the traits the father contributes is the sex of the child. There are two kinds of sperm cells, one, called a Y sperm, determines a male offspring and another, called an X sperm, determines a female. The male apparently predominate over the female: for every one hundred girl babies born in the world, one hundred and six boys are born.

The dowry of heritage from father and mother is in the nucleus of each parent cell.

The father's nucleus is in the head of the sperm. The mother's is in the middle of the egg. In each nucleus there are units called genes; at least fifteen thousand genes in each. The genes are so small that they cannot be seen through any microscope, but they are the remarkable packages of chemical instructions for the design of each and every part of the new baby. The "instructions" are inscribed in the genes by the molecules of their content which is a nucleic acid called DNA. If one imagines the molecules to be symbols, like an alphabet, then one can imagine how these molecule "letters" composed in varying sequences can spell out different instructions in each gene.

When the sperm nucleus reaches the egg nucleus these two lie side by side as their content is combined. In this half hour an immeasurable number of traits of the new baby are decided within the pin-point egg. These include the features of the human species and also the individual trademarks such as male or female sex; the color of eyes, hair and skin; the configuration of face and body; the tendency to be tall or short, fat or lean, ruggedly healthy or prone to some diseases; and undoubtedly also the tendency to certain qualities of temperament and intelligence. With so many genes joined when the parent cells unite, there is obviously vast possibility for new variety of the existing family patterns. Each new baby is a unique individual, never entirely like either parent or any ancestor.

As the synthesis of the two different parent

nuclei is completed within the single egg, two new nuclei arise. The genetic make-up of these two new nuclei differs from that of either parent: it is a blend of both. That moment, when the two new nuclei form and the now fertilized egg divides in two, is the beginning of the life of a new individual. This is zero hour of Day One.

In the last moments before conception the two parent nuclei (dark spheres in the egg) are combined. Interior of egg is here revealed by transmitted light.

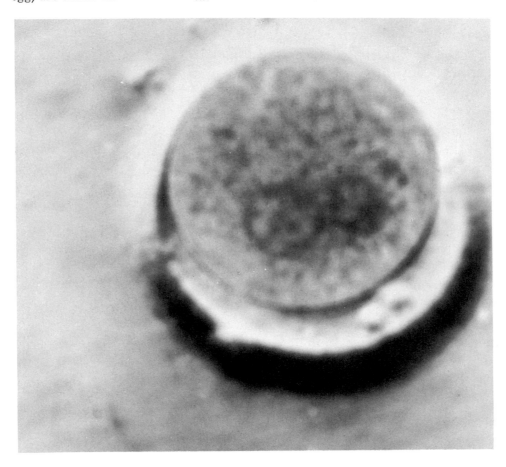

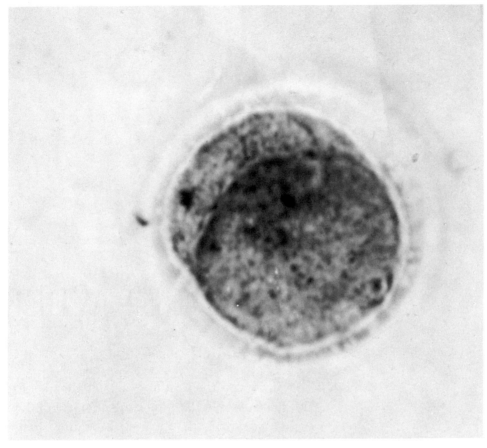

The first day of a baby-to-be begins when two cells like these arise from the single egg.

In this book, the age of the baby will always be computed from this beginning. But this hour is so difficult to establish for any individual that prenatal age is usually dated from the mother's last menstruation. Physicians speak of menstrual, not actual, age in pregnancy. The Chinese, by ancient custom, declared a child to be one year old at birth. They long ago acknowledged that we are not new at birth.

27

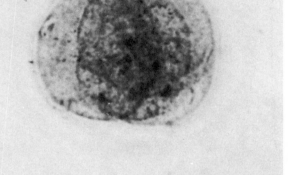

TEN HOURS after the first two cells there are four.

THE FIRST WEEK

In one week the first two cells of the new life increase, two by two, to more than a hundred cells. Together, they are still smaller than a period and are still bound by the barely stretched pellucid membrane, the same that held the single egg. For the first three or four days of the first week the cluster of cells drifts slowly downstream in the tube that leads to the womb. On about the fourth day the cluster arrives in the uterus. There it continues to drift about for another two or three days. Then, by the week's end, the cluster becomes attached to the inner lining of the womb and will remain firmly implanted there until birth.

The womb is usually well prepared to receive the cluster of cells. In its thimble-sized

28

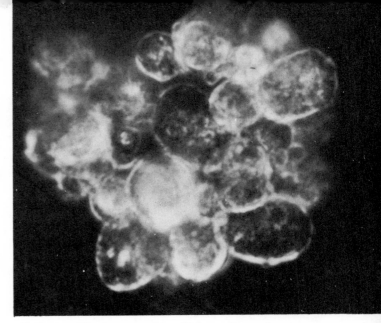

TWO DAYS later there is a "mulberry" cluster. The larger cells will form the embryo.

cavity it contains a watery fluid rich in sugars and salts. The free-floating cell cluster may absorb some nourishment from this and is also protected by the fluid from becoming crushed. When the floating cell cluster is ready to become implanted, the inner lining of the uterus is ready to provide a fertile ground. This is the special function of the menstrual cycle, a cycle which regularly renews and replenishes the tissues of the womb. The cycle starts after each menstruation when the newly stripped lining of the uterus begins to regenerate to become a thick spongelike surface. This makes an ideal bed for an implanting cell cluster because the spongy tissues are rich in the blood supply that will be essential to a growing embryo. When fertilization does not take place within the month, the menstrual cycle ends with menstruation, which is the disintegration and shedding of the built-up tissues. It has been called the weeping of a

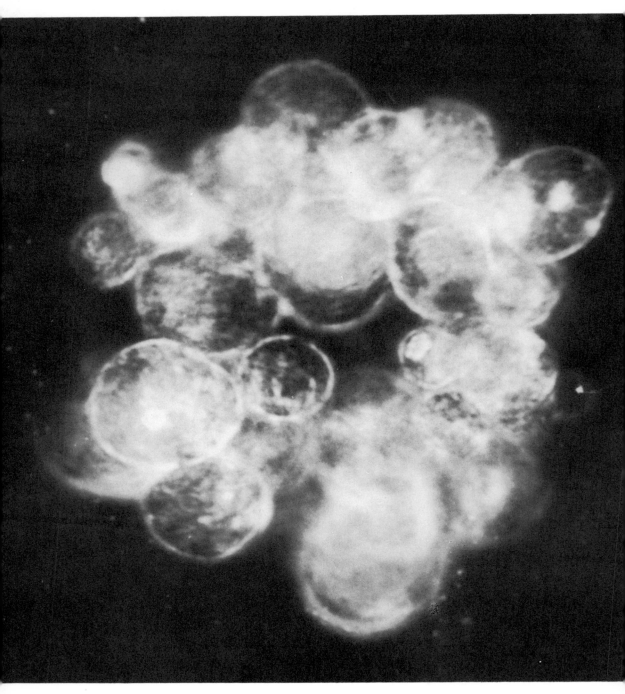

SIX DAYS old, an incipient human would have about one hundred and fifty cells, beginning to form a hollow cluster and about to seek a place for nesting in the womb.

disappointed uterus. When the uterus is not disappointed, menstruation is suppressed through a change in the maternal hormone balance, and the spongy lining continues to build up throughout pregnancy to maintain a hospitable environment for a baby.

When the four-day-old cell cluster arrives in the womb, it is made up of about three dozen cells. These have become closely packed together and are technically known as a morula (from the Latin for mulberry). The cells of the "mulberry" resemble the earliest cells of all creatures: invertebrates, fish, fowl and mammal. But the resemblance is superficial. On microscopic examination, the human cells differ from the cells of other animals in small details, about as much as two watches of different makes differ from one another. From their first hour the human cells are distinctly human.

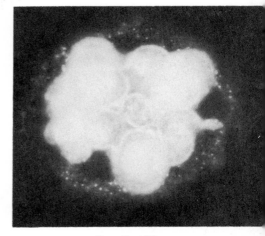

THREE DAYS after fertilization the cluster is closely packed and has about three dozen cells still enfolded in the pellucid zone.

How do these early human cells propagate, not their own kind, but the vast variety of highly specialized cells that will perform the diverse functions of all the parts of the human body? We do not yet fully understand the mechanism that controls the specialization of the different cells, but we do know that the "instructions" packaged in the genes of each cell spell out a master code. As the cells gain in number, the blueprint is passed on from cell to cell. But the new cells do not follow the entire instructions. Each responds only to a part of the master code—some to one part and some to another. It is in this way that many of the new cells become different from their fel-

The lining of the womb here is spongy and prepared to receive an embryo. In the center of the photograph is a "nested embryo."

low cells. In the language of the embryologist, the cells become differentiated. The three dozen cells of the mulberry are already differentiated. Some are smaller than others. The smaller ones will initiate the growth of the tissues that will be discarded at birth, such as the "afterbirth," and the outer membranes that will nourish and house the growing baby. The larger cells will produce the embryo itself. In anticipation of this, the larger cells soon become differentiated from one another. One larger-cell layer will produce all the specialized cells of the brain, spinal cord, nerves and skin. Another layer will be the foundation for the digestive system, the liver and the pancreas. The third layer will become the skeleton, the heart, the blood vessels and the muscles.

While the mulberry drifts about in the fluid of the uterus, its three dozen cells increase to about one hundred and fifty differentiated cells. In the process the solid cluster of the mulberry becomes hollow at its center. It is now called a blastocyst (from the Greek *blastos,* meaning sprout, and *cyst,* meaning pouch). On the sixth or seventh day, perhaps in need of new food resources, the "sprout pouch" settles down, usually along the upper curvature of the uterus, and begins to burrow into the

The capsule in which the cell cluster becomes an embryo rises like a plateau from the uterus.

spongy inner lining. This is called "nesting." In the process of nesting, tiny blood vessels are broken in the maternal tissues. The bits of broken tissue and the spilled droplets of maternal blood are nourishing for the growing cells. The cells absorb the nutrients, just as a plant absorbs nourishment from the wet soil. In fact, the human cluster soon grows a fine network of roots, called villi (the Latin word for tufts of hair). In addition to gathering nourishment, the villi also serve to implant the cell cluster firmly in the uterus.

If we could look into the womb at this time with a magnifying glass, we would see a spongy, pale-lavender surface, and on it a tiny blister encircled by crimson. The translucent blister is the baby-to-be. The crimson wreath is the slight wound caused by the invasion into the maternal tissues. By the end of the first week the maternal tissues begin to heal over the invader and form a scarlike capsule over the cell cluster. The cluster gains extra protection thereby. Within the opaque walls of the capsule a spectacular metamorphosis will take place. Soon the cluster of cells, increasing and changing every hour, will be transformed into a distinctly human creature with a head and body, arms and legs, fingers and toes.

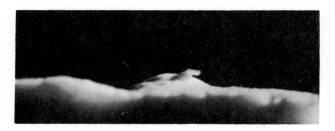

Another view of the embedded capsule shows an extra tab of maternal tissue formed in the healing process.

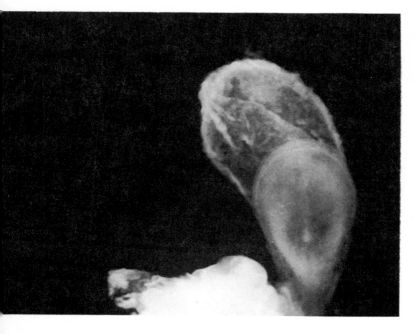

IN THE SECOND WEEK the new cells build an "embryonic shield" and a balloon-like sac above it. The shield has preliminary tissues for a whole body; most of its wide top is the precocious brain region. The sac is called a yolk sac, although it contains no yolk and no nutrients. Its relationship to a true yolk sac, like that of birds, is only in its appearance.

THE
FIRST MONTH

ON THE NINTH DAY an embryo begins to take shape in the cluster of cells that is now well nested in the womb. In the days that follow the cells increase from hundreds to many thousands and turn into the highly specialized components of a human body. Each kind of cell is marshaled into its proper place as a body emerges, day by day. On one day, the twenty-fourth day, the embryo has no visible arms or legs. But forty-eight hours later, the

IN THE THIRD WEEK the body unfolds. It is one-tenth of an inch long; the heart begins to beat; the brain has two lobes; the early spinal cord is bordered by the future vertebrae and muscle segments.

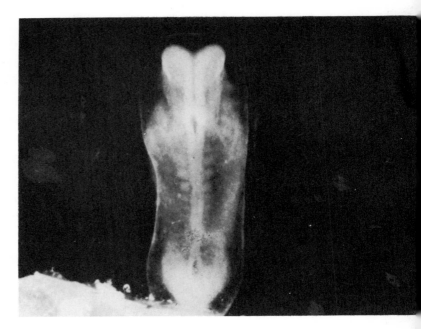

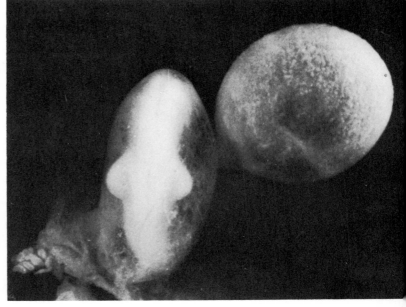

IN THE FOURTH WEEK the body is almost a quarter of an inch long. It has head, trunk, and arm buds. The "bag of waters" grows with the embryo. The non-functional yolk sac (right) will soon diminish in size but may remain as a small lump of useless tissue until birth.

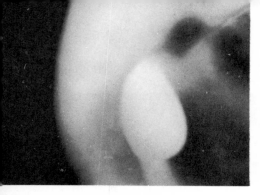

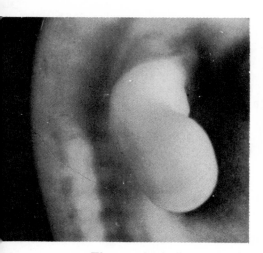

The arm buds illustrate the rapid pace of growth: Near the end of the month they are simple knobs. Two days later, upper and lower arm are formed. Three days later there are hand "plates" with finger outlines (see page 48).

beginnings of arms, tiny buds at the sides of the body, are suddenly there. The legs make their first appearance two days later, always lagging slightly behind the arms in development until the third year of life.

By the end of the first month a whole embryo is formed. From head to heel it is a quarter to half an inch long. It is the size of half a pea, fragile as jelly and almost without substance. One can hardly see the fine detail of its structure. But the body has a head with rudimentary eyes, ears, mouth and a brain that already shows human specialization. There are simple kidneys, a liver, a digestive tract, a primitive umbilical cord, a blood stream and a heart. The heart is usually beating by the twenty-fifth day. It is only a primitive heart, a U-shaped tube two millimeters long. But the twenty-five-day-old embryo is so small that the minute heart forms a large bulge on its body. This heart, in proportion to the size of the body, is nine times as large as the adult heart. After a few days of practice it pumps sixty-five times a minute to circulate the newly formed blood that is needed to nourish the embryonic tissues. The blood flows through the embryo in a simple closed system of vessels that is separate from the mother's blood circulation.

The month-old embryo has come a long way from its beginning but it does not yet look very human. It appears to have a tail; it has ridges along the side of the head that suggest gill slits; it has arm and leg buds that do not look much like human arms and legs. It is sometimes said that the human embryo "recapitulates the evolutionary history of man" and resembles first a fish, and later perhaps a monkey, before becoming a baby. This is not true. The alleged gills are never gills and the tail is not a tail. The extension that looks under magnification like a tail is actually no larger than the head of a pin. The apparent tail encloses the early spinal cord, which, in anticipation of the elaborate human nervous system, is temporarily longer than the rest of the body. It will eventually become the tip of the adult spine, called the coccyx. The alleged gills are not openings and have no gill fronds. They are five folds of tissue that pile up at the base of the head to provide raw material for the chin, cheeks, jaw and for the external ear. A human embryo superficially resembles the

The month-old embryo, three times enlarged here, has a large head with folds that may be mistaken for gills but are material for ears and jaws. The minute tip of the spinal cord may be mistaken for a tail. The embryo lies in the capsule whose luxuriant roots provide anchor and nourishment. The small round mass at the left is the yolk sac which has become widely separated from the embryo.

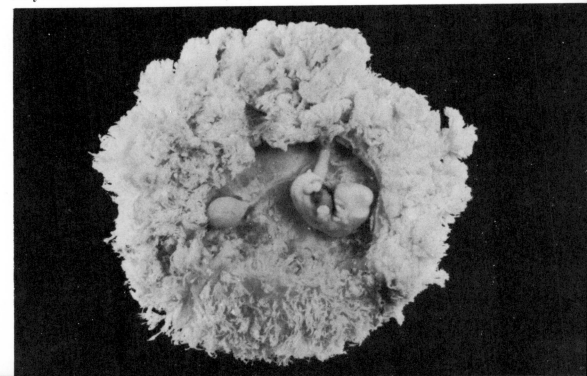

embryo of a fish and monkey and other animals because all embryos grow from one-celled eggs and are made, step by step, out of the building blocks of cells. Nature's repertory of basic structure is limited, and the same forms appear in all the primary units of building blocks. Thus, the gills in fish develop out of similar folds of tissue as the jaw of man. The tail of a monkey grows out of the same stub that becomes our coccyx.

The simple structure is soon changed. Development moves ahead each day and progressively molds the embryo more and more into an individual. In the earliest stages of growth every embryo has only those simple parts needed for immediate survival. These are followed in time by increasingly complex organs that anticipate the final form dictated by the genetic master code in the cells. The constantly increasing numbers of cells become increasingly more diverse and specialized. They must be regimented and organized into a body. Each kind of cell must grow at the right time and at the right place. Many years of investigation in biology have been devoted to the study of this organization. The most recent findings indicate that there is a strong interaction, probably a chemical communication between the cells. The interaction first of all keeps cells of a kind together. For example, all kidney cells exercise some control on one another. In addition there is an interaction among the various groups of cells so that they develop in an integrated way. Each group of cells responds to the requirements of the other groups. Each organ functions only in relation to the other organs.

Dr. George W. Corner, in his book *Ourselves Unborn,* gives a vivid analogy to the progressive system of organization: "Imagine a little workshop started by one man of all-around talents. His first employees learn the business from him and as the factory grows they become department heads, each organizing his own part of the work until all sorts of specialized workers are developed, capable in their turn of developing new employees but only in their own narrow fields."

The embryo is a self-contained unit, a biological workshop or factory. To some extent it creates its own environment. For example, its delicate tissues must constantly be bathed in fluids or they would wither and be crushed. The organizers of the early cell cluster anticipate this. Even before an embryo is formed, some cells gather to make a transparent bubble. Fluid seeps into the bubble from the surrounding maternal tissues and it becomes the fluid-filled chamber in which the embryo, and later the growing baby, lives in the womb. This bubble, known as the "bag of waters," is the amnion (which means little lamb in Greek). The word was chosen because lambs are often born enclosed in their prenatal membranes. While the embryo grows under the direction of its own organizers, it depends entirely on the mother for nourishment. In this first month the nourishment is gathered by the hundreds of rootlike tufts that cover the capsule which encloses the transparent amnion and the

The root-covered capsule that is embedded in the womb and houses the embryo in the first and second months.

embryo within. The food is channeled from the roots to the embryo through a stalk that is a primitive umbilical cord.

By the end of the month the embryo completes the period of relatively greatest size increase and greatest physical change of a lifetime. The month-old embryo is ten thousand times larger than the fertilized egg was. The single egg has given way to a finely structured if still incomplete body. In four more weeks, by the end of the second month, it will look quite like a tiny baby.

The opened capsule shows the embryo in its fifth week. In a week or two it will look much more like a baby. This embryo has a primitive umbilical cord through which food, gathered by the roots, is channeled to the embryo.

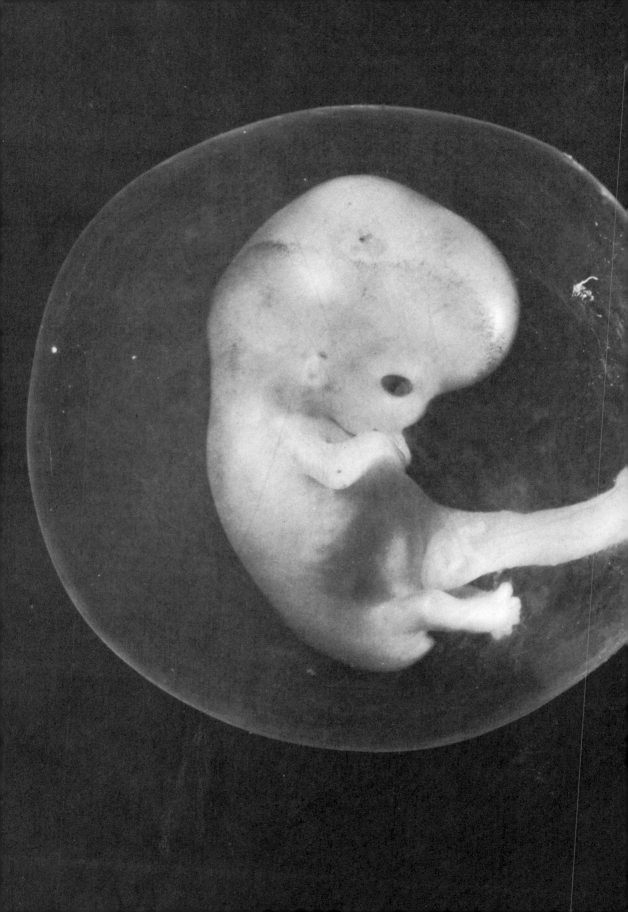

THE SIXTH WEEK. Life-size.

THE
SECOND MONTH

IN THE FIRST THREE WEEKS of this month the primitive embryo becomes a well proportioned, small-scale baby. In its seventh week it bears the familiar features and all the internal organs of the future adult, even though it is less than an inch long and weighs one-thirtieth of an ounce. It has a human face with eyes, ears, nose, lips, tongue, and even milk-teeth buds in the gums. The body has become nicely rounded, padded with muscles and covered by a thin skin. The arms, only as long as printed exclamation marks, have hands with fingers and thumbs. The slower-growing legs have recognizable knees, ankles and toes.

IN THE SEVENTH WEEK the embryo is completed. This photograph is about seven times life-size. One week earlier (above), the body was still unfinished; the arms shorter; toes, and also the ears, were unformed.

43

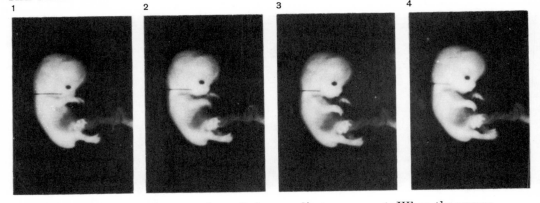

Motion-picture films in the seventh week show earliest movement. When the upper lip, the first sensitive area, is stroked with a fine hair (1–3), the back muscles con-

The new body not only exists, it also works. The brain, in configuration already like the adult brain, sends out impulses that co-ordinate the functioning of the other organs. The heart beats sturdily. The stomach produces some digestive juices. The liver manufactures blood cells and the kidneys extract some uric acid from the blood. The muscles of the arms and body can already be set in motion.

When the embryo reaches such completion safely and without impairment, it has a good start in life. Now it is ready to enter the next phase of development. Until adulthood, when full growth is reached between the years of twenty-five and twenty-seven, the changes in the body will be mainly in dimension and in the gradual refinement of the working parts.

It is perhaps unfortunate that the existence of the incipient individual is still largely unnoticed and often unappreciated during the crucial weeks of the formation of the body. It may be unfortunate because, like a tender

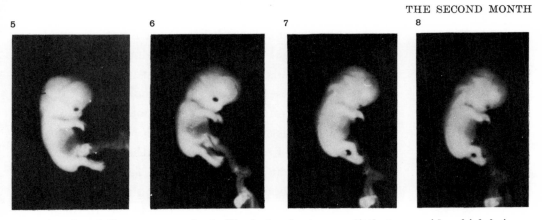

tract and the arms move back. The body also turns a little to one side which brings the left leg down (7, 8). The photographs are slightly larger than life-size.

seedling, the new life is vulnerable. During this period of teeming cell growth necessary for the building of the body, the new cells are especially susceptible to all physical and chemical influences, good and bad. When an embryo fails to grow properly, nature, one might say benevolently, tends to erase the incipient error through miscarriage in the very first weeks of pregnancy, often before the pregnancy is recognized. In this period, diseases of the mother can be communicated to the embryo. The most susceptible parts of the embryo are always those that are growing most rapidly at the time of the infection. For this reason the virus of German measles, for instance, may affect different tissues of the embryo at different stages of growth. This is an important reason why mothers in early pregnancy should avoid exposure to known communicable diseases. They should also, if possible, avoid exposure to X rays, because it is known that radiation can penetrate to the embryo.

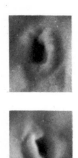

The ears take shape in the fifth and sixth weeks. They form out of two folds of tissue. One fold, the left one, becomes the ear shell and lobe; the other makes a partial cover over the open ear canal.

The great susceptibility of germinating cells probably has an important biological advantage: it tends to make the cells respond to the instructions from the genes and from other cells. The effectiveness of the communication is well illustrated by the development of the ears in the first and second months, and by the development of the hands and feet. The two ears develop in unison, in timing and in form. The same is true of the two hands and, in turn, of the two feet. At the same time every embryo, as soon as it has ears, hands and feet, has individual ones shaped according to the family pattern. In the seventh week some embryos have larger ears than others, some have prominent earlobes, others almost no lobes. The hands and feet show their individuality mainly in the lines of the skin on palms and soles. At two months the lines of the palm prints and footprints are already permanently engraved on the skin.

Under the direction of the genes, the embryo emerges in individual form, but usually with little individual variation in the timing of the development. The embryo is like a clockwork. Each part is accurately geared to every other part. Each also arises in a universally fixed sequence. The time schedule for the formation of the body is generally so consistent that it has been possible to set down the agenda of development for each day of the first forty-eight days of life. An embryologist looking at an embryo during this period could tell precisely how old it is from the stage of formation of the body.

According to the daily agenda of development, we find that the embryo grows one millimeter a day. But it does not grow in even progress throughout the body; different sections move ahead on different days. On Day 30 (plus or minus one day, allowing for the minor variations found in all living things), the arm buds are tiny rounded knobs on the sides of the body. On about Day 31, the arm buds become subdivided into hand, arm and shoulder regions. On about Day 33, the hand section begins to show the finger outlines. On the same day the eyes are dark for the first time because pigment has just formed in the retina. The brain on this day is one-fourth larger than it was two days earlier. In ten more days it will have, in miniature, the complex structure of the mature brain. Also on Day 33, the wide-apart nostrils begin to show elevated rims that are the beginnings of the formation of the nose and upper jaw. Four days later, on Day 37, the tip of the nose shows up in profile. The two nostrils have moved closer together and a nose is fully formed with two separated air passages. On the same day the internal hearing apparatus of the ear nears completion. The eyelids just begin to form as ridges around the rims of the eyes. One week later the eyelids have grown to cover almost all the eyeball. This is Day 44. The embryo has now acquired a good upper and lower jaw and a definite mouth with lips, a beginning tongue, and the initial buds for the twenty milk teeth embedded in the gum ridges.

The embryo is no longer quite the insub-

In the seventh week the outer ear is well molded. The inner hearing mechanism is also almost completed.

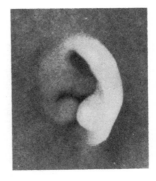

1

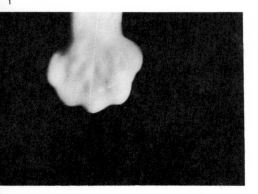

2

stantial creature of the first month. In the sixth week it has gained a complete skeleton. The skeleton is not yet made of bone. It is fashioned of cartilage, like the tip of the adult nose. Between Days 46 and 48 the first true bone cells replace the cartilage, always in the bones of the upper arms.

The appearance of the first bone cells marks the end of the embryonic period. This criterion has been chosen by embryologists because the beginning bone formation coincides with the essential completion of the body. Now perfection of function will follow perfection in structure. As the embryo (from the Greek, to swell, or teem within) becomes a fetus (from the Latin, young one, or offspring) near the close of the second month, it can well be called a baby. He or she is now a little person.

THE HANDS grow from a "plate" with finger ridges in the fifth (1) and sixth weeks (2). In the seventh and eighth weeks (3) fingers, thumbs, and fingerprints form. The prominent touch pads regress in the third month (4).

3

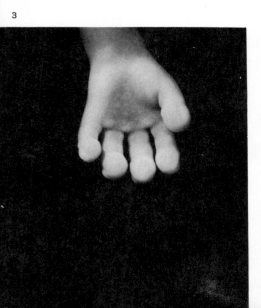

4

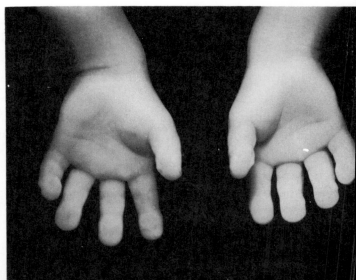

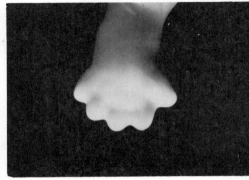

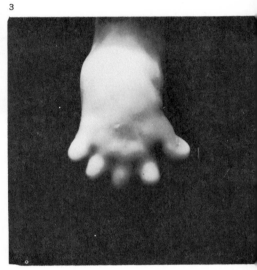

THE FEET follow the hands and begin in the sixth week (1), and forty-eight hours later (2) have larger toe ridges. The heel appears by the end of the week (3) and grows out in the next five days (4). The prominent walking pads regress in the third month (5).

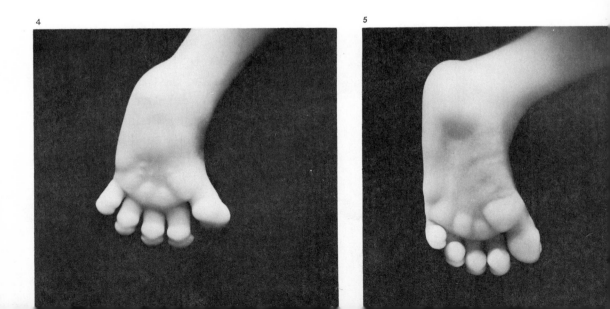

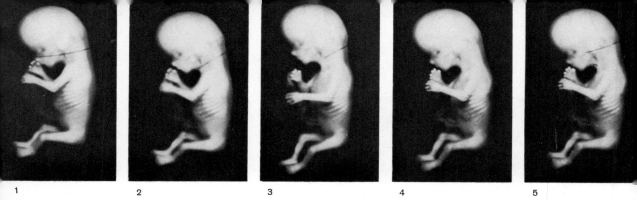

MOTION IN THE NINTH WEEK—When the lip area is brushed with a hair (1), the muscles of the back and neck respond (3). This causes a slight raising and turning of the head, a motion of the arms, and a hip movement that lowers the left leg. The

THE THIRD MONTH

In this month the baby begins to be quite active, although he is still so small that he could easily move about inside a goose egg, and weighs only one ounce. By the end of the month he can kick his legs, turn his feet, curl and fan his toes, make a fist, move his thumb, bend his wrist, turn his head, squint, frown, open his mouth and press his lips tightly together. He cannot yet purse his lips for sucking, but he can, and frequently does, swallow. He will swallow considerable amounts of amniotic fluid from this time until birth. He may even breathe. Long before the breathing-control center of his brain and the tissues of his lungs are ready to assume effective respiration of air, he begins to practice the inhaling and exhaling movements. These send amniotic fluid in and out of the primitive lungs. This aspira-

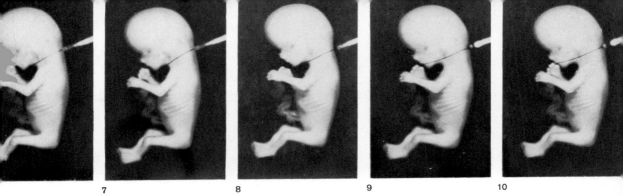

7   8   9   10

baby returns to his resting position (4, 5). When the palm of the hand is brushed (6), the fingers close down partially (7) in one of the first localized responses. The arms, formerly stiff, now bend. These photographs are slightly smaller than life-size.

tion of fluid may be essential to the proper formation of the lungs' air sacs. The baby does not drown because of this, as he would after birth, since he does not depend on his lungs for air. His oxygen supply comes from his mother through the umbilical cord.

The mother, with rare exceptions, does not yet feel her lively baby. His newly formed muscles are weak. He is so very small that the womb is barely expanded and is still contained within the girdle of the hipbones. In another month, in the sixteenth week, the enlarging uterus will rise out of the hipbone confines, the baby will be much stronger, and the mother will begin to feel him turning and kicking against her sensitive abdominal wall. These first-perceived movements are known as the "quickening," which was once thought to mark the actual beginning of a life in the womb.

How do we know that the baby moves before his stirrings are felt by the mother? It has been possible to detect the movements with delicate shock-recording devices placed on the

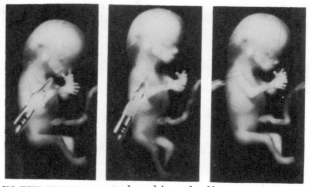

IN THE TENTH WEEK brushing the lip area causes a vigorous straightening that includes the legs.

mother's abdomen. It has also been possible to observe the baby's earliest activities. The embryologist Davenport Hooker, with several associates at the University of Pittsburgh, compiled thousands of feet of motion-picture film over a period of thirty years. These films have recorded the activities of babies born very early, some as early as the sixth week of life. All the photographs in this book that show the movements of the baby are taken from these films. The films make an important contribution to science, for they have clearly established that prenatal behavior grows, just as the organs of the body grow, in orderly progression and according to a genetically determined pattern.

Two prerequisites for motion are muscles and nerves. In the sixth and seventh weeks, nerve and muscle work together for the first

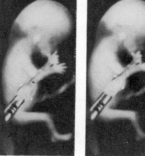

The fingers close down when the palm is brushed but do not yet form a real fist.

time. If the area of the lips, the first to become sensitive to touch, is gently stroked, the baby, who then is still an embryo, responds by bending the upper body to one side and making a quick backward motion with the arms. This is called a "total pattern" response because it involves most of the body rather than the appropriate local part. Localized and more appropriate reactions, such as swallowing in response to a stroking around the lips, follow only in the third month. By the beginning of this third month the baby moves spontaneously, without being touched, for the first time. Sometimes, his whole little body swings back and forth for a few moments. A few days later, by eight and one half weeks, the eyelids and the palms of the hands become sensitive to touch. If the eyelid is stroked, the baby now has a localized reaction and squints. If the palm of the hand is touched, the fingers close to a partial fist. In two more weeks he will be able to close his fingers better, but only at twenty-three weeks will he be able to grip firmly. After birth, when he learns purposeful motion, his ability to pick up objects, at will, grows in the same sequence as his prenatal skills : at first the baby will reach out and make a partial fist; then he will learn to make a good fist; and only later will he be able to hold on to what he wants.

In the ninth and tenth weeks his abilities

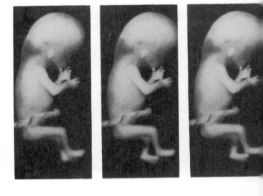

The leg responds for the first time to a touch on the sole of the foot.

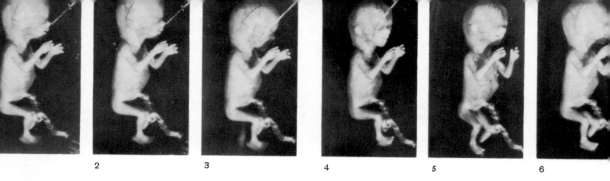

1   2   3   4   5   6

IN THE TWELFTH WEEK motion becomes specialized and graceful. If the lips are stroked the baby may close the mouth tightly (2) and swallow (3). He may also respond with a "smile" (5, 6) that is the beginning of the sucking reflex. The hands can co-ordinate to move toward one another (7–9). When the sole of the foot is

take a leap ahead. This progress is made possible because the number of nerve-muscle connections in the body increase almost threefold in these ninth and tenth weeks. Now, if the baby's forehead is touched, he may turn his head away and pucker up his brow and frown. By this time, the baby has the full use of his arms and can bend elbow and wrist independently. In this same week the entire body becomes sensitive to touch with a notable exception: the sides, back and top of the head. The back and top of the head will remain totally insensitive until after birth, which could be nature's way for protecting the head in birth.

The twelfth week again brings a whole new range of responses. The baby can now move his thumb in opposition to his fingers. He begins to be able to swallow. He can also pull up his upper lip in what looks like a lopsided sneer but is actually the initial step in the development of the sucking reflex. Yet he still does not turn his head toward anything that touches his mouth, as he will when he gets older. His behavior now is often seemingly designed to avoid rather than to seek—a fact that is not yet well explained.

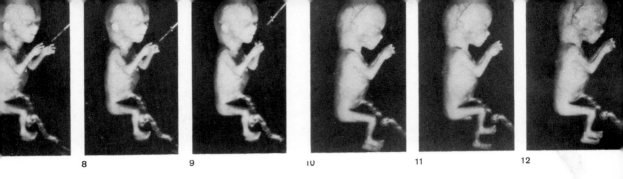

tickled, the baby kicks one leg and draws up the other. When hand and foot are touched simultaneously, only the hand responds. The baby cannot act on two separate stimuli, and the upper body dominates the lower in response. This tends to be so until the fifth or sixth year of life.

When the twelfth week ends, the baby reaches a milestone. In his book, *The Origin of Overt Behavior,* Davenport Hooker states: "... this is an important age landmark, as the quality of response is altered. It is no longer marionette-like or mechanical ... the movements are now graceful and fluid, as they are in the newborn ... the fetus is active and reflexes are becoming more vigorous." All this, before the mother feels the movements!

Every baby shows a distinct individuality in his behavior by the end of his third month. This is because the actual structure of the muscles varies from baby to baby. The alignment of the muscles of the face, for example, follows an inherited pattern. The facial expressions of the baby in his third month are already similar to the facial expressions of his parents. But inherited qualities are not the only factors that determine what he can do and how he does it. His environment in the womb apparently plays a part. In a report on "Early Human Fetal Behavior," Davenport Hooker notes: "In the normally developing organism, behavior is an expression of inherited structure.... It is well known that maternal diet or certain diseases suffered by the mother may prenatally alter structure. Where these early changes in structure seriously affect the neuro-muscular mechanism, alterations in behavior may be expected."

As we have seen at the close of the previous chapter, the physical structure of the baby was essentially complete by the end of his second month. Still, the third month brings important new refinements. Some of these are nice finishing touches. For instance, the nail beds form on the finger tips and will soon bear little fingernails. The baby's face becomes much prettier. His eyes, previously far apart, now move close to the bridge of the nose. The eyelids close over the eyes by the ninth week and temporarily seal them like a newborn kitten's eyes. They will remain closed until the sixth month, when the baby will be able to open them. The ears, formerly low on the head, now move upward to eye level. Meantime, the ribs and vertebrae turn to hard bone as the whole baby becomes more solid. Girls and boys begin to look distinctly different now. The girl's external vulva and the boy's penis both have gradually become molded out of nearly identical folds of tissue during the second and third months. In this time, the internal reproductive organs also become well formed and already contain some primitive egg and sperm

Girls (left) and boys (right), can easily be distinguished in the third month but the differences are indeed small. In girls, labia will grow to enfold the protuberance that appears large now. These photographs are four times life-size.

cells, the forerunners of the cells that will make future babies.

The vocal cords are completed. In the absence of air they cannot produce sound; the baby cannot cry aloud until birth, although he is capable of crying long before.

At birth the baby must be ready to suck and take in food. In this month his body makes many special preparations for this. On the mouth the sensitive lips are formed, and the sucking muscles of the cheeks fill out. The taste buds and the saliva-producing glands appear, and the two halves of the hard palate, the roof of the mouth, come together and fuse. The palate is a bony plate that divides mouth from nose and makes simultaneous eating and breathing possible. People who have a cleft palate, sometimes in conjunction with a harelip, have it because these parts failed to fuse properly at three months.

The three-month-old baby has working digestive glands in his stomach. When the baby swallows amniotic fluid, its content is largely utilized by his body. In exercising his functions the baby also begins to urinate occasionally. The drops of urine are sterile and are carried away in the regular exchange and freshening of the amniotic waters.

In anticipation of the time of birth, the baby steadily improves and rehearses the vital functions of breathing, eating and motion. But before he can be fit for the rigors of independent life, he must become much larger and much more solid. In the next, the fourth, month he will make great strides in this direction.

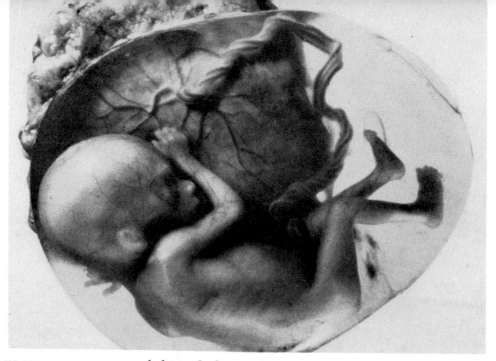

IN THE FOURTH MONTH, baby and placenta are nearly equal in size but the baby will soon become much larger.

THE

FOURTH MONTH

In THE FOURTH MONTH the baby grows so much that he reaches half the height he will have at birth. In only four weeks he increases his weight sixfold and adds well over five inches to his length. He becomes eight to ten inches tall, but even after the rapid weight gain, weighs only six ounces.

For this prodigious growth the baby must take in a good deal of sustenance: food, oxygen and water. This comes to him from his mother through the placenta. The placenta (also called

Baby, placenta, and uterus form a unit. The umbilical cord leads into the placenta and the placenta is attached to the lining of the pear-shaped uterus.

afterbirth) is the organ through which all supplies flow to the baby until birth. Its name, placenta, is the Latin word for cake. It is "cake" for the baby, and it is also formed somewhat like a cake. It is rooted in the lining of the uterus. At four months it is a little over three inches in diameter. By birth, when it will become detached to be discarded, it will have grown to an eight-inch diameter and will weigh about one pound.

The placenta is a very potent organ and it is unique in its versatility. It alone can perform the diverse functions of the adult lungs, the kidneys, the intestines, the liver and some of the functions of a hormone gland. In addition to all this, it also produces substances that can combat infections. The placenta carries out the functions of the adult lung in this way: within the placenta carbon dioxide leaves the baby's blood stream and is exchanged for oxygen brought to the placenta by the mother's blood stream from her lungs. The baby's blood flows into the placenta through his umbilical cord and his blood never leaves the closed vessels of the cord. The mother's blood never directly enters into the cord. The exchange of carbon dioxide for oxygen, of wastes for nutrients, is carried out across the porous walls of the closed blood vessels.

Life in the womb has once been described as "Everest *in utero*" because in these months the baby requires relatively little oxygen. But if the mother should happen to be temporarily low on oxygen, perhaps through anesthesia, or because of a trip without benefit of a pressurized airplane to unaccustomed high altitudes, the baby may suffer a shortage also. If a mother permanently lives at high altitudes, the placenta will compensate for this. It will grow to be larger than an ordinary one. The placenta carries out the functions of the kidneys, the liver, and the intestines in this way: in the placenta, as in the kidneys, urea is filtered out of the baby's blood and is carried away by the mother's blood stream to her kidneys to be eliminated. In the placenta, as in the adult liver, some of the mother's blood cells are processed and components such as iron are transferred to the baby. In the placenta, as in

The prenatal tree of life is formed by the vessels of the placenta. They are here removed from their covering tissues. The two white stems in the foreground are the arteries that carry the blood out of the umbilical cord. These branch into a closed network that returns the circulation to the cord in the single large vein that is the darker stem in the foreground. In the branching vessels, wastes from the baby are traded for nutrients from the mother.

the adult intestines, food molecules are processed by digestive enzymes so they can pass
into the baby's blood vessels. At the same time
digestive wastes are filtered out of the baby's
blood in the placenta and carried away in the
mother's circulation.

In the fourth month the placenta becomes a
main source of the hormones necessary to the
mother's body in pregnancy and to prepare
for the production of milk. Later, it will have
an important part in determining the changing hormone balance that helps to bring about
labor and birth.

In addition to all this, the placenta may serve
to keep mother and baby healthy. It can syn-
thesize globulins, natural blood ingredients
that can prevent infection. The globulins are
dispersed mainly to the baby but the mother
probably receives some as well, especially in
the last three months of pregnancy.

The baby's link to the placenta is the umbilical cord. The placenta and the umbilical cord
develop only in man and in those animals that
do not hatch from eggs. Through these two
structures the baby can be a self-contained
unit while he is completely dependent on his
mother. His whole body functions as a closed
system. He has his own blood circulation,
pumped by his heart, which at four months
pumps the equivalent of about twenty-five
quarts a day. (By the time of birth his heart
will pump three hundred quarts a day.)

The umbilical cord was formed in the embryo. It extends from the baby's navel and
grows with him. By the time he is big enough

to be born, the cord will average two feet in length but may vary from five inches to over four feet. It will be capable of carrying about three hundred quarts of fluid a day. This courses through a closed loop of vessels embedded in the cord. They are embedded in a jellylike substance that fills the cord. This is called Wharton's jelly. It has a light bluish-green color that shines through the pale sheath of the cord. In the cord two arteries carry used blood out from the baby. They carry the blood through the placenta where wastes are traded for sustenance as the blood, through connecting links of thousands of branching vessels, is returned to the baby. It travels back through one large vein that enters at his navel and sends fresh blood on another round through his body.

The umbilical cord is so well engineered that the blood stream within travels at four miles an hour and completes the round trip through cord and through the baby in only thirty seconds. There is a special advantage to the fact that the blood travels with such force. The force distends the cord and gives it the consistency of a water-filled garden hose. Like a filled hose, the cord resists knotting and tends to straighten itself out if it becomes tangled as the baby moves about. Therefore, the cord is rarely a knotted cord.

Mother and baby have separate blood. The mother's blood stream never directly enters the umbilical cord, but what he receives through the cord is entirely determined by his mother's resources. She takes care of her baby by taking care of herself. He can receive only as much food, as much of vitamins, calcium and other essentials, as she has to share. In the physics of exchange across the walls of his blood vessels, he cannot completely deplete her supply. The old saying that "baby takes all" is not true. However, even if the mother is not eating well during her pregnancy, her body will carry reserves if she has been reasonably well nourished before. Also, her biological efficiency is so much stepped up during pregnancy that even mothers who are seriously undernourished have been known to give birth to nine-pound babies. Substances that enter the mother's blood stream are transferred to the baby so readily that he receives them within an hour or two. If she has an alcoholic drink, the baby will get some of it too, although this has not been found to be harmful. If she smokes a cigarette, some nicotine will reach the baby.

Unfortunately, the old belief is not correct

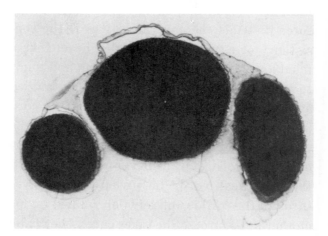

The umbilical cord in cross section, at birth, shows the two arteries and one larger vein still distended by the flow of the circulation.

that the placenta provides a barrier to screen the baby from all undesirable substances. The walls of the umbilical vessels do act as a filter and keep out large particles like whole proteins, whole red cells and most bacteria. But the walls are like a barnyard fence, that is, impermeable to horses but permeable to mice. Thus the smaller particles, the components of the large ones and also all gases pass through easily. This is why the anesthetics used in childbirth anesthetize the baby also; and why the agents of infections can be transferred from mother to baby. By the same token, drugs like penicillin or sulfa that may be used to treat the mother treat the baby as well, and all the immunities which the mother acquires are also transferred to the baby. He will soon become immune to many diseases, and the immunities will last for some months after he is born. This is one reason why the next five months spent in the womb will be such an important preparation for birth.

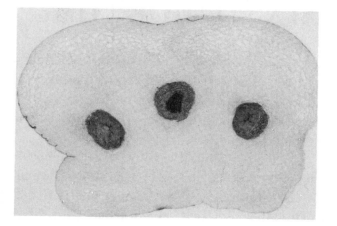

Immediately after birth the blood circulation through the cord ceases naturally before the cord is cut, because the jelly content of the cord swells up and constricts the blood vessels.

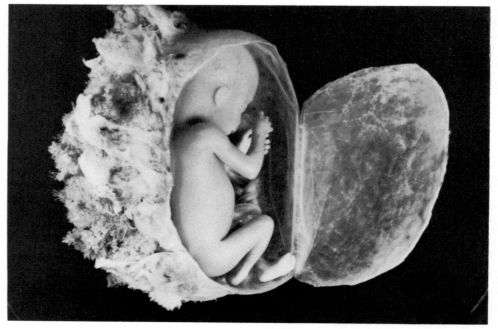

AT THE BEGINNING OF THE FIFTH MONTH

THE FIFTH AND
SIXTH MONTHS

An ARRESTED MOMENT of life is recorded in its
perfection in these photographs, reminiscent
of sculptured cameos. This is a baby at the
outset of his fifth month, still enclosed in the
translucent amnion.

In the fifth month the baby gains two inches
in height and ten ounces in weight. By the end
of the month he will be (about) one foot tall
and will weigh one pound. Fine baby hair

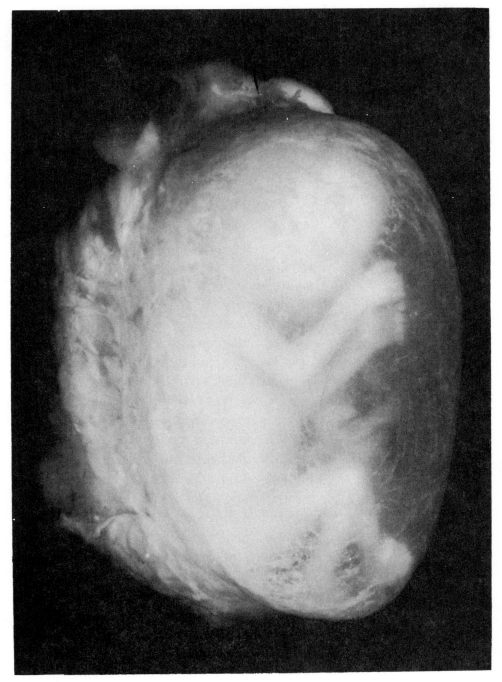

LIFE-SIZE

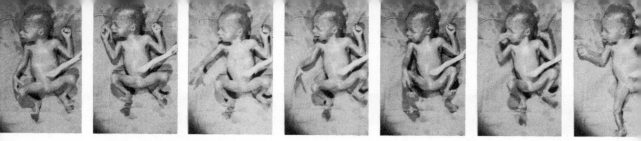

AT THE BEGINNING OF THE SIXTH MONTH motion-picture films show that the baby can cry, suck, make a fist and that his behavior is remarkably mature. His kicks and

begins to grow on his eyebrows and on his head, and a fringe of eyelashes appears on his still-closed lids. In another month the hair on his head may even be long. Girls and boys now both develop pale pink nipples and also the underlying mammary glands, and these are equipped with milk ducts. Most of the skeleton hardens. Hard nails form on the nail beds of the fingers and a little later on the toes. In the eighth month the fingernails will reach the tips of the fingers. At the time of birth they will probably extend beyond the fingers and be in need of trimming.

In the fifth month the baby's heartbeat is louder. If he lies in a favorable position it may be possible to hear the heart with an ear to the mother's abdomen. With a stethoscope it can be heard well. If there are twins, the physician may be able to pick up the sound of the two hearts. The baby's muscles become much stronger, and as the baby becomes larger, his mother finally perceives his many activities. Usually, she detects a slight flutter of movement late in the fourth or early in the fifth month. In very rare instances, especially if she is a slim woman, she may feel this much earlier. Soon the commotion turns into a definite kicking and turning. If she learns to recognize the different parts of his body, she will be able to distinguish hand from foot, and head

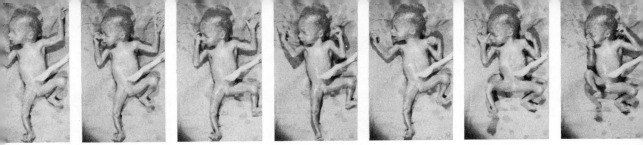
punches are now plainly felt by his mother but he is still so small that he has room to turn somersaults in the womb.

from buttocks. At times she may even feel a certain knocking, like a series of slight rhythmic jolts, fifteen to thirty a minute. This means that her baby is hiccuping. Babies have hiccups in the womb and these may last from a quarter hour to half an hour.

The baby sleeps and wakes much as a newborn does. When he sleeps he invariably settles into his favorite position, called his "lie." Each baby has a characteristic lie. Some always sleep with the chin resting on the chest, while others tilt the head back, sometimes as far as it will go. When he awakens he moves about freely in the buoyant fluid, turning from side to side and frequently head over heel. Sometimes his head will be up and sometimes down at this age. He will keep this up until the ninth month, when he no longer has much elbow room. He may sometimes be aroused from sleep by external vibrations. He may wake up from a loud tap on the tub when the mother is taking a bath. A loud concert, or the vibrations of a washing machine, may also stir him into activity.

In the sixth month the baby will grow about two more inches to become fourteen inches tall. He will also begin to accumulate a little fat under his skin and will increase his weight to a pound and three quarters. This month the buds for his permanent teeth come in, high in

Every baby has his "lie," his favorite position for sleep now and later.

his gums behind the milk teeth. Now his closed lids can open, and he may open and close his eyes and look up, down and sideways. He develops such a strong grip that he will soon be able to support his weight by holding on to a rod with one hand. Most importantly, in the sixth month he can maintain regular breathing for some twenty-four hours if born prematurely. He may even have a slim chance of surviving in an incubator. The youngest babies known to have survived birth were between twenty-three and twenty-five weeks old and weighed about one pound. But usually the baby's breathing mechanism and his lungs, and also his digestive system, are still too immature to take over their full functions.

When the baby is born so early, he is small and emerges easily. He often remains enclosed in the unruptured amnion, as did the baby in the photograph on page 67. The amnion, though transparent and hardly thicker than the paper of this book, is tough and slightly elastic, like sausage casing. Unlike sausage casing, it is quite lovely and has a natural silvery shimmer. It is a living tissue made up of a single layer of skin cells. As the baby grows, the amnion adds new cells and grows also. It is always a closed bubble and forms a water-tight seal around the umbilical cord which protrudes through it.

Although the amnion is watertight and per-mits no liquid to leak out, the amniotic fluid is by no means a stagnant water. In fact, it has been found in recent years that more than a third of its volume is removed and replaced every hour. This means a total daily exchange equivalent to six gallons in volume! Where does the fluid come from and where does it go? We do not yet know the full answer. The main sources of the incoming fluid appear to be the baby's own lungs and kidneys. It has been found that the lung and kidney tissues normal-ly produce considerable amounts of fluid. A secondary source is the amnion itself. The liv-ing skin cells of this sheath also produce some fluid. In addition, some of the water molecules and molecules such as salts and sugars trav-erse the sheath and enter from the cavity of the uterus. The regular outgoing of the fluid

IN THE FIFTH AND SIXTH MONTHS the grip becomes strong. This baby is holding a rod and moves his arm up and down as the rod is moved.

71

is still less well explained. Some, perhaps a great deal, may be swallowed and utilized by the baby. The amniotic fluid gradually increases in the early months to more than one quart by the fifth month. The volume remains the same until the seventh month, when a natural readjustment reduces it by one half, leaving more room for the much bigger baby. The quantity then remains stable until birth.

The amniotic waters have an evolutionary significance. Through them the higher forms of life make the transition from a marine existence to dry land. The waters that protect the fragile embryo later cushion the growing baby against blows. They also keep the baby at an even temperature of body warmth. They support him so that he is virtually weightless and this facilitates his exercising. He can roll over now as he will not be able to do in his crib until some months after birth. But the long submersion might be hard on his skin. He is protected from this and from abrasion by a thick whitish cream produced by his own skin and covering it like the coat of grease of a channel swimmer. The cream is called vernix (the Latin for varnish).

In these two months a fine woolly fuzz called lanugo (the Latin for wool) appears—especially on the arms, legs and back. Most of this falls out before birth. It may be an evolutionary reminder of man's fur-bearing ancestors. Two other features that may hark back to man's prehuman ancestry appear in the fifth and sixth months: as taste buds are formed on the tongue and inside the cheeks, they crop up in

IN THE FIFTH MONTH the baby is still very small compared with the size of an adult hand. This baby, the same that gripped the rod on the previous page, can move about freely, buoyed by fluid as he would be in the womb.

an abundance found in many animals. In the human they diminish in number before birth and never increase again. The baby's grip is another curious feature. As it is perfected in the sixth and seventh months, it is more powerful than that of the infant soon after birth. But if the baby is fed from the breast his ability to grip is reinforced and remains strong for a while longer. This is thought to suggest that the baby develops an instinctive grip like that of monkeys who, in suckling, must be able to hold on to their mother's fur.

When the baby reaches six months he has completed two-thirds of his stay in the womb. In the coming three months he will become progressively able to live without such an intimate life line to his mother.

THE SEVENTH, EIGHTH AND NINTH MONTHS

In these three months the baby gains most of his birthweight and outgrows his home in the womb. He usually puts on more than a pound in the seventh month and will probably gain four more pounds in the following six weeks.

In the seventh month the hair on the baby's head may grow long and most of the downy lanugo is shed from his body. He may begin

 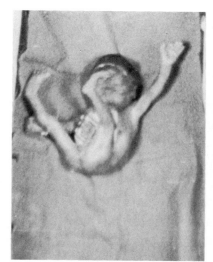 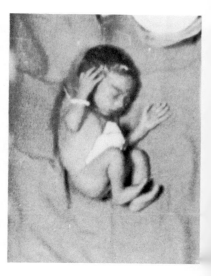

74

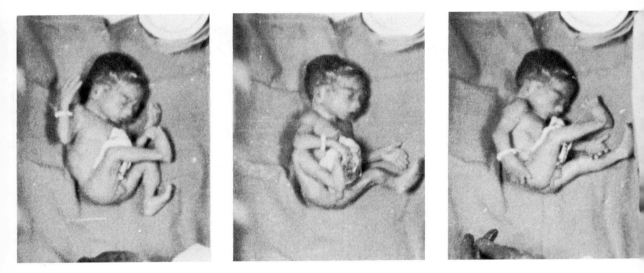

EARLY IN THE SEVENTH MONTH this baby, weighing one pound and fifteen ounces, was born healthy and strong. In films taken immediately, the baby demonstrates the activities that are usually felt but not seen.

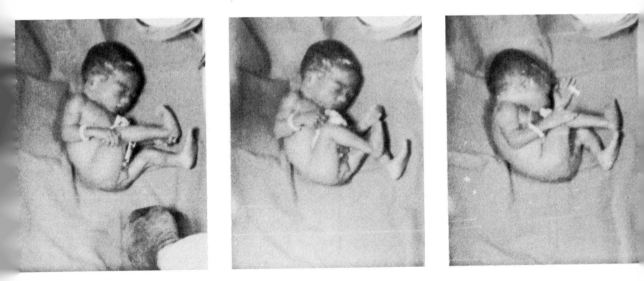

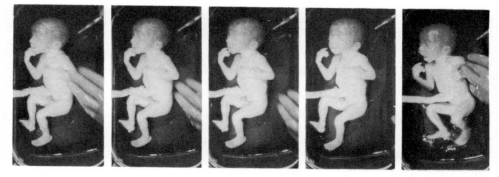

BY THE SEVENTH MONTH he may be sucking his thumb in the womb. This baby tries his finger, loses it, and cries.

to practice sucking and may already suck his thumb. Some babies are actually born with a callus on the thumb from sucking it in the womb.

In the eighth month he gains at least two pounds, mostly in a protective padding of fat that will help to keep his body warm after birth. He may even become quite chubby if his mother overeats at this time. Even with a normal weight gain, he fits so snugly into the womb toward the end of the month that he can only turn from side to side and can no longer turn somersaults. It is likely that he will now settle into a head-down position. Most babies do, probably because the head is the heaviest part of the body and is best accommodated in the bottom contour of the uterus.

In the ninth month his quarters become even more cramped. When he moves, the contours of his arms and legs make moving bulges on the abdomen of his mother. A kick from the baby in the womb has been known to almost knock a book off the mother's lap.

When the mother lacks the resources to fill the increasing needs of the baby, he may be born ahead of his time. Statistics show that this happens most frequently for reasons that are social and economic. Poor nourishment, poor health and very hard work are some of the main causes of premature birth. Twins are also often born early. This is thought to be simply the result of lack of space. When the uterus can expand no more, the babies are born.

Late in the seventh month most babies reach a weight of two and a quarter pounds and in medical language become viable, which means "with organs sufficiently formed to enable them to live if born." These babies still lack the important heat-insulating layer of. fat mentioned earlier and acquired in the eighth month. They must always be cared for in a heated incubator, to shelter them from tem-

The premature infant needs constant care and the even heat of an incubator. Here a physician checks heartbeat, respiration, and temperature. This baby weighed two pounds at birth.

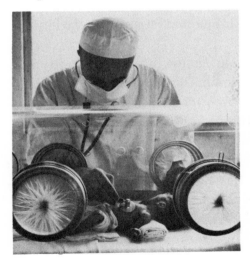
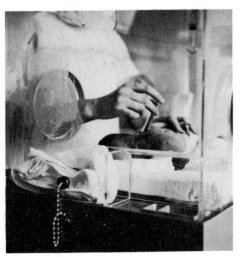

perature change and protect them from infection.

Even with the best medical attention, the baby that is already so strong and lively in the womb is set back by premature birth. He will be a frail creature in an incubator. His existence is often precarious, for he may still have great difficulty in breathing. Even if he can maintain breathing, his lung tissues may not yet be sufficiently formed to absorb the necessary quantity of oxygen. His digestive system may not function well and he will inevitably lose weight at first. He will also be extremely vulnerable to infections.

The baby mothered in the womb gets a good deal more than warm, sterile accommodations and a well regulated supply of oxygen and predigested groceries. In these last three months in the womb he also gets one of the most essential ingredients for survival. From his mother's blood, from the placenta, and also perhaps from the amniotic fluid which he swallows, he receives substances that will endow him with immunity to a wide variety of diseases.

By the ninth month the baby is hardy because many immunities are transferred to him in the last three months before birth. From the blood of his mother he receives the special disease-combating proteins called antibodies. She has specific antibodies in her blood against all those diseases (but only those diseases) which she has had and to which she has acquired some immunity. Among them may be measles, chicken pox, mumps, whooping cough, scarlet fever, the common cold, some strains of streptococci and influenza and also poliomyelitis. If the mother has been effectively vaccinated against smallpox or poliomyelitis, she will carry antibodies against these diseases and her baby will be protected against them as well. His protection is good but not perfect. It may be helped by the mother's antibodies that will be in her milk, especially in the watery colostrum that comes in before the milk. But it has not been established whether antibodies can be absorbed through a baby's stomach, as we know they are in many domestic animals. The immunities a baby acquires from the mother before birth will gradually wear off and disappear within about six months. By that time the baby's own system can cope better with infections and can begin to build up its own permanent immunities. A girl baby will in time be able to pass these on to the next generation.

While the baby generally benefits from his mother's antibodies, there is at least one kind that can cause trouble—those related to the Rh factor. This Rh factor is so named for the *Rh*esus monkeys that were used in the studies of the problem. The problem can, but does not always, arise when an Rh-negative mother, one who has no Rh factors in her blood, carries an Rh-positive baby—one who has inherited these Rh factors, from an Rh-positive father. In such a case, antibodies may be formed in the mother to combat the Rh substance that the baby has introduced into her body. These antibodies may cause trouble for both mother and baby. The same principle can apply to some other blood incompatibilities between mother and baby. We are today learning more about these and how to treat them effectively.

In addition to antibodies, the baby receives another substance that is very effective in combating diseases. This is gamma globulin. Some comes from the mother. Most of it is produced by the placenta and it is shared by baby and mother. It probably helps to make the mother more immune to diseases during the last three months of pregnancy.

In the last month before birth, the baby will have a level of antibodies and gamma globulin in his blood which at least equals his mother's. In this and all other respects, he is coming to the point where he has reaped the full benefit of this totally dependent way of life. Nature begins to make preparations for birth. The mother feels the "lightening," as her expanded uterus sinks about two inches downward in her body. When this happens, the "presenting part" of the baby becomes engaged in the tight-fitting circle of pelvic bones. The head (or buttocks) from then on remains firmly wedged at the entrance of this bone tunnel through which he must make his exit. Now he is really pinned down.

The baby usually stops growing by his two hundred and sixtieth day, about a week before birth, probably because the placenta ages and loses much of its efficiency. The aging of the placenta also brings about the change in the maternal hormone balance which aids in setting off the mechanism of labor. The mechanism works so well that 75 per cent of all babies are born within eleven days of the appointed 266 in the womb. The number of days is small compared to the extent of change. In quantity the change involves numbers so large as to be almost meaningless. One cell has become two hundred million cells before birth, and these cells weigh six billion times more than the fertilized egg. Although the initial pace of growth slows down long before birth, the baby, if he continued to grow even at the slowed rate of his ninth prenatal month, might weigh one hundred and sixty pounds on his first birthday. At the prenatal rate, he would be twenty feet tall on his twentieth birthday and his weight would be many million times that of the earth. Fortunately, man increases his weight only about twenty times from birth to adulthood.

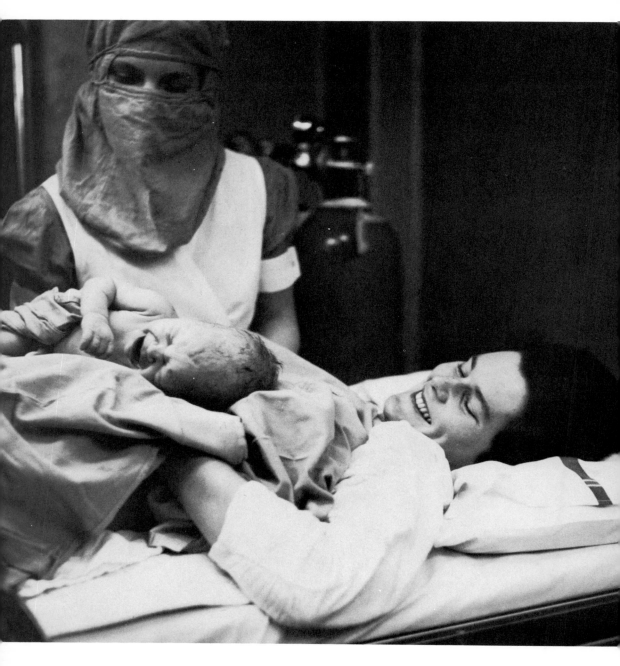

THE
DAY OF BIRTH

... no more their wonted joys afford
the fringed placenta and the knotted cord.
Oliver Wendell Holmes

BIRTH IS BEAUTIFULLY ARRANGED by nature to bring together the needs of the baby and the capacity of the mother. It is well timed. The baby becomes mature enough to be born just when he is so large that the womb is stretched to its limits. Yet he is still barely small enough to get out through the narrow birth passage. He has no more room to move and no more room to grow. His growth is actually arrested a few days before birth because he gets less food from the aging placenta. The aging of the placenta and the response of the womb muscles to the great stretching will now help to set in motion the spectacular process of labor and delivery.

When he is ready to be born, the baby may weigh less than six pounds or more than ten pounds, depending on his inherited body design and on the nourishment provided by his mother. If he weighs under five pounds and

TWO MINUTES after birth the nine-month-old baby gives a hearty cry as he begins to breathe. The cord is not yet cut; the head is distinctly "molded" from the exit through the tight birth passage.

eight ounces, he is considered to be premature in development, regardless of his presumed age. If he weighs more than ten pounds, he is either too fat or he may be postmature. His birth may have been delayed and he may be older than nine months. The average baby weighs a little over seven pounds and is twenty inches long. Boys are somewhat bigger than girls.

The head of the baby has a circumference about equal to that of his shoulders or buttocks. It is usually a tight fit for the opening of the bone-enclosed outlet through which he must travel. Fortunately, the head of the baby has some "give." His skull is not yet fully solid. It is made up of five large bone plates, which are still separated and can be pushed together. Between the plates there are narrow spaces that expose the tough membrane, the dura mater (in Latin, hard mother), that protects the brain. The spaces between the bone plates are called the sutures because, months later, when the skull plates are solidly joined, the lines of juncture look just like a stitched seam. The sutures of the newborn baby are also called fontanels (which means little fountains) because the pulsing of the baby's blood stream can be plainly felt over them. The best known of the fontanels is the "soft spot" on top of the baby's head.

The fontanels give the head its needed flexibility. Just before, and especially during birth, when the head is pressed hard against the birth canal, it gradually becomes molded as the bone plates slide together and sometimes come to overlap slightly. The natural molding does not damage the brain. It safely reduces the diameter of the skull and gives it the characteristically elongated shape of the newborn head. A few days after birth the head will regain its rounded form.

Birth is never easy for the baby. It may take less than an hour or it may last many hours. The average duration of the birth of a first baby is fourteen hours. The average duration of the birth of subsequent babies is eight hours. Dr. Samuel Reynolds, a biologist who has studied the mechanics of labor, has said that like the three R's of education there are three P's of labor. They are: the Passage, the Passenger and the Power. To these, one might add another: Psychology. Certainly, attitudes are involved in the progress of birth. The length of labor, the welfare of passenger and mother will depend on these three, and perhaps four, P's.

The first thing that happens in birth, sometimes shortly before, is a narrowing of the uterus, which results in straightening the baby's body so that his head (or, in a few cases, his buttocks) is pressed against the outlet of the womb, called the cervix (in Latin, neck). Next, the virtually closed cervix must give way to accommodate the width of the baby's head. It has been established that the muscles of the top of the uterus apply a force comparable to a weight of fifty-five pounds to the baby with each contraction. Usually, the amnion ruptures under this pressure and, depending on the size and location of the tear, the fluid either rushes or trickles out. The contractions coming at increasingly frequent intervals push the baby against the cervix until the passively resisting muscles of this outlet give way and the head of the baby can slip out as through a tight bathing cap.

This completes the first and longest stage of birth. The second stage is quicker but requires much greater force. To move the baby out to his crowning, as the birth of the head is called, a force equal to a weight of nearly one hundred pounds is needed. The extra power must be supplied by the efforts of the mother. This is why the process of birth is called "labor." When the mother's muscle power, for various reasons, is not sufficient, the physician must help. He must work to bring the baby out by the pull of forceps or sometimes even by Caesarean birth. Both can be lifesaving procedures but they are not preferable to the more gentle process of nature.

The baby's condition in birth will be quite parallel to that of his mother. If she has a difficult time, he will also. If she is groggy from medication, he will have received the medication through the placenta, and he will be a sleepy baby. If she is wide awake, he will be too. He will make continuing breathing efforts on his way out and will breathe on his own and be lively on arrival.

The first breaths of air are the hardest in life. It has been calculated that the first breathing-in requires five times the effort of an ordinary breath because the air must be drawn in to expand the thousands of tiny uninflated air

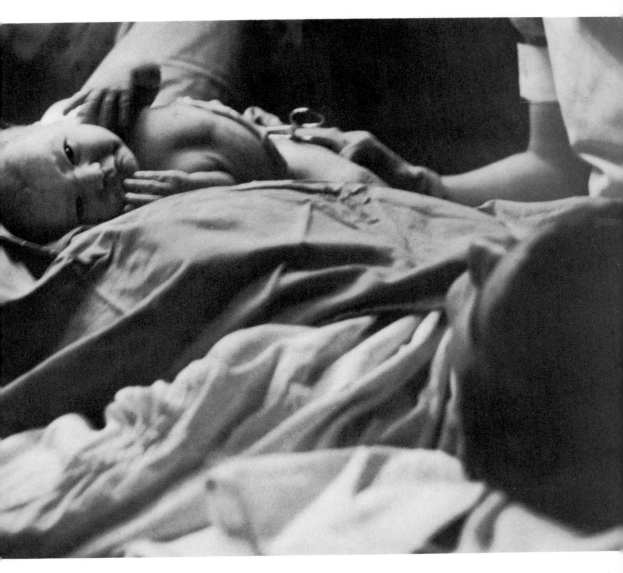

FOUR MINUTES after birth this wide-awake baby appears to be taking a look at his mother. His umbilical cord has just been cut.

sacs of the lungs. It is an effort that can be compared to blowing up a rubber balloon. Breathing only gradually becomes easier. It continues to be irregular for two or three days. It takes that long to clear the air passages of mucus. For this the early cries are useful, for they help to clear out obstructing fluids. The cries may be a reflex response or they may be an expression of the baby's discomfort. He has good reason to be uncomfortable. He is wet and he has just come into a room that is about 20 degrees colder than the 98-degree womb. It is also bright after the darkness and his eyes, although they are still in poor focus, can distinguish light.

At the same time, major adjustments take place in the baby's body as the route of his blood circulation changes radically. His blood stops flowing through the umbilical cord as soon as the cord is born. As he draws his first breath, his heart must begin to pump blood to the lungs to pick up oxygen. Now a major valve must close inside the heart to keep used and fresh blood separated.

The baby must begin to breathe and get his oxygen within minutes after birth. He receives the last oxygen-laden blood from the placenta as he emerges. The circulation is cut off in the umbilical cord when it is exposed to air. Nature closes the cord through a special jellylike substance that is packed around the three blood vessels in the cord. This jelly swells up with exposure to air and compresses the embedded vessels just as a tourniquet would. When the physician cuts the cord, it is a practically bloodless cut done only for convenience. The whole cord, with the placenta attached at its far end, would dry up and drop off naturally within a week or so, leaving the usual healed scar, our navel. The placenta is usually born very soon after the baby. It is detached from its moorings as the uterus rapidly contracts in size. Cord and placenta have outlived their usefulness at birth.

One of the pleasant aspects of the baby in birth is that he arrives quite clean. He is wet from the amniotic waters but not bloody. The first thing the mother traditionally looks for is to see whether her baby is a boy or girl. Whether boy or girl, she will find that the external organs of sex are swollen. In a boy only the scrotum will be swollen; in a girl the lips of the vulva. This is an inconsequential and only very short-lasting effect of the long umbilical relationship the baby has had with the mother. The special hormones of pregnancy that were circulating through her blood stream were shared to some extent by the baby. Those hormones that made her birth canal more elastic have made the baby's genital tissues distended. Other hormones that stimulated the enlargement of the mother's breasts and prepared them for milk production have stimulated the baby's breasts. Boys and girls alike actually have milk in their breasts for a few days after birth. This is called "witches' milk" and it sometimes drips from the nipples of the newborn. Thus, even boys have working mammary glands at one time in their lives.

From the womb the baby will bring with him some vernix cream still collected in the pockets of his skin folds. He may still have some downy lanugo hairs on his forehead, back or shoulders. These will fall out soon. His skin will be light, regardless of his race. Negro babies and all babies are light at birth. The pigments that color the skin are not yet in force and will not be for several days or even weeks. His abdomen is big and round because his liver is large from the special functions it has had in the production of blood cells. His nose may be runny from accumulated amniotic fluid. His ears are plugged with mucus so that he cannot hear. The mucus will clear out in a day or so, and then his hearing may be supersensitive for a while. His face may have some scratch marks from his own long fingernails, which will probably be in need of immediate trimming. His eyes will have no tears, no functioning tear ducts for several weeks. The first cries are always tearless ones. His eyes open and close and move about at random, sometimes staring, then again scanning the scene, often with some lack of co-ordination so that, at times, the baby may look walleyed or cross-eyed. He can distinguish light and dark and sees something of large shapes and moving objects.

From the womb the baby may bring the habit of sucking his thumb. He is able to suck vigorously now. If anything touches his cheeks, fat from well developed suck-pad muscles, he will turn toward it and seek food. If anything touches the palm of his hand, his

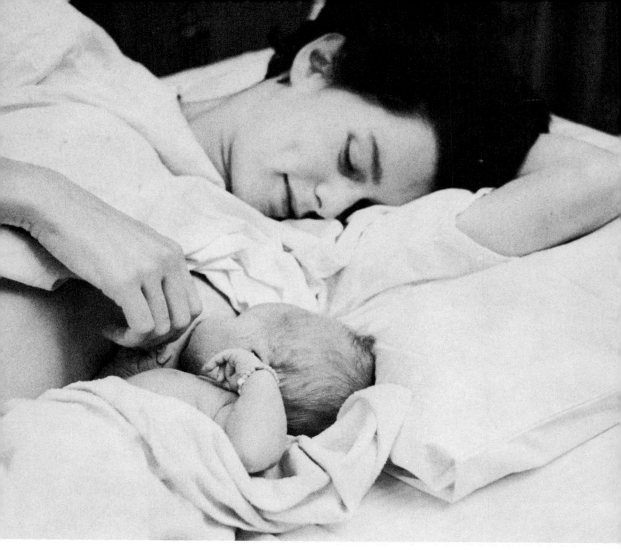

FIFTEEN MINUTES after birth the baby puts to use his long practiced sucking. He gets colostrum, the fluid which precedes milk. Some babies are awkward at first at the breast.

fingers close down in such a tight grip that he could even support his own weight if suspended by his hands. If his feet touch solid ground while his body is firmly supported, he will make stepping movements that are often mistaken for precocious walking. If he is laid on his tummy, he will make some swimming-like, primitive crawling efforts.

ONE HOUR after birth baby and mother look at the father who stands beside the bed.

It is surprising how soon after the first shock of birth the baby begins to act thoroughly at home in his new environment. As soon as he is dried and warmly wrapped in a blanket, he will cough and yawn and sneeze and ogle his new world. If put to his mother's breast he tries to suckle and usually succeeds soon. Then his liveliness subsides; he draws up his legs and arms to the position he favored in the womb and drops off into a very long, sound sleep to recover from this hard day.

ACKNOWLEDGMENTS

I am greatly indebted to the investigators in biology and other fields related to prenatal development who have recorded their information in writing and often in photographs. These sources are gratefully acknowledged below and on the following pages. I would like particularly to express my appreciation here to all who so generously made their photographs available to me.

In the preparation of the manuscript numerous friends and acquaintances have helped immeasurably in showing their interest and giving needed advice. Of those who read the manuscript for clarity and accuracy I would like to mention, most especially, Dr. George W. Corner who kindly reviewed the entire text. Also, Dr. Davenport Hooker who reviewed the text, in particular the sections on the development of motion. Miss Freda Parks and Mr. Horace Hughes have been very helpful as well in their review from the point of view of the Maternity Center Association.

Mrs. Eve Metz of Simon and Schuster deserves special credit for the very creative job she has done in the design of the layout for the many photographs.

THE PHOTOGRAPHS

The author wishes to extend her thanks to the following for their kind permission to use these photographs:

University of California Medical Center (p. 61)

By courtesy of the Carnegie Institution of Washington (pp. 42-43)

and by courtesy of the following individuals: Harold Cummins (pp. 48-49), Richard Grill (pp. 66-67), Arthur T. Hertig and John Rock (pp. 31, *bottom,* 32-33), Chester H. Heuser (p. 34), Chester H. Heuser and George W. Corner (p. 35, *top*), Milo Herrick Spaulding (p. 56), George L. Streeter (pp. 36, 47), Chester Reather (pp. 16-17)

Davenport Hooker and Tryphena Humphrey, *from* the physiological and morphological studies on human prenatal development, Department of Anatomy, University of Pittsburgh School of Medicine (pp. 44-45, 50-55, 68-71, 73-76)

David Linton (pp. 82, 84, 87, 91, 92) Reprinted with permission of McGraw-Hill Book Company, Inc., from *Understanding Natural Childbirth* by Herbert Thoms, Laurence Roth, and David Linton (photographer). Copyright © 1950, by McGraw-Hill Book Company, Inc.

Eugen Ludwig, Anatomisches Institut der Universität Basle (pp. 35, *bottom,* 37, 46)

Edith L. Potter (pp. 58-59) By permission from *Fundamentals of Human Reproduction* by E. L. Potter. Copyright 1948, by McGraw-Hill Book Co., Inc.

Samuel R. M. Reynolds (pp. 64-65)

David Seymour—Magnum (p. 77)

Landrum B. Shettles (pp. 18-21, 26-30, 31, *top*) from *Ovum Humanum,* 1960 by Hafner Publishing Company, Inc., New York. Also (pp. 22-23, 40-41).

MAIN SOURCES OF INFORMATION

MEDICAL TEXTBOOKS

Arey, Leslie Brainerd, *Developmental Anatomy*, 6th ed. Philadelphia, W. B. Saunders Company, 1954.

Eastman, Nicholson J., *Williams Obstetrics*, 11th ed. New York, Appleton-Century-Crofts, Inc., 1956.

Greenhill, J. P., *Obstetrics*, 11th ed. Philadelphia, W. B. Saunders Company, 1955.

Patten, Bradley M., *Human Embryology*, 2nd ed. Toronto, Blakiston Company, Inc., 1953.

BOOKS AND MONOGRAPHS

Corner, George W., *Ourselves Unborn, An Embryologist's Essay on Man.* New Haven, Yale University Press, 1944.

Darwin, Charles, *The Descent of Man, and Selection in Relation to Sex.* London, John Murray, 1871.

Dibner, Bern, *Darwin of the Beagle.* Norwalk, Connecticut, Burndy Library, 1960.

Gesell, Arnold, *The Embryology of Behavior.* New York, Harper & Brothers, 1945.

Hooker, Davenport, *The Origin of Overt Behavior.* Ann Arbor, University of Michigan Press, 1944.

—, *A Preliminary Atlas of Early Human Fetal Behavior.* Pittsburgh, Published by the author, 1944.

—, *The Prenatal Origin of Behavior.* Kansas, University of Kansas Press, 1952.

Potter, Edith L., *Fundamentals of Human Reproduction.* New York, McGraw-Hill Book Company, Inc., 1948.

Shettles, Landrum B., *Ovum Humanum.* New York, Hafner Publishing Company, Inc., 1960.

Toverud, Kirsten, Stearns, Genevieve, and Macy, Icie G., *Maternal Nutrition and Child Health.* Bulletin of the Nat'l. Research Council, No. 123, 1950.

Villee, Claude A., ed., *The Placenta and Fetal Membranes.* Baltimore, The Williams & Wilkins Company, 1960.

Windle, William F., *Physiology of the Fetus.* Philadelphia, W. B. Saunders Company, 1940.

RESEARCH

Congdon, E. D., "Transformation of the Aortic Arch System during the Development of the Human Embryo." *Contributions to Embryology,* Vol. XIV, No. 68 (1922).

Corner, George W., "Well-Preserved Ten Somite Embryo." *Contributions to Embryology,* Vol. XX, No. 112 (1929).

Cuajunco, Fidel, "Development of the Motor End Plate." *Contributions to Embryology,* Vol. XXX, No. 195 (1942).

—, "Development of the Neuromuscular Spindles." *Contributions to Embryology,* Vol. XXVIII, No. 173 (1940).

Cummins, Harold, "The Topographical History of the Volar (Walking) Pads in the Human Embryo." *Contributions to Embryology,* Vol. XX, No. 113 (1929).

Hertig, Arthur T., and Rock, John, "On the Preimplantation Stages of the Human Ovum." *Contributions to*

Embryology, Vol. XXXV, No. 240 (1954).

—, "Two Human Ova of the Previllous Stage, Having an Ovulation Age of about Eleven to Twelve Days." *Contributions to Embryology,* Vol. XXIX, No. 184 (1941).

—, "Two Human Ova of the Previllous Stage, Having an Ovulation Age of about Seven to Nine Days." *Contributions to Embryology,* Vol. XXXI, No. 200 (1945).

Heuser, Chester H., and Corner, George W., "Developmental Horizons in the Human Embryo, Four to Twelve Somites." *Contributions to Embryology,* Vol. XXXVI, No. 244 (1957).

Heuser, Chester H., Rock, John, and Hertig, Arthur, "Two Human Embryos Showing Early Stages of a Definite Yolk Sac." *Contributions to Embryology,* Vol. XXXI, No. 201 (1945).

Hooker, Davenport, "Early Human Fetal Behavior, with a Preliminary Note on Double Simultaneous Fetal Stimulation." *Proceedings of the Association for Research in Nervous and Mental Disease,* Baltimore, The Williams & Wilkins Company, 1954.

Menkin, Miriam, and Rock, John, "In Vitro Fertilization and Cleavage of Human Ovarian Eggs." *American Journal of Obstetrics and Gynecology,* Vol. 55, No. 3 (March, 1948).

Reynolds, Samuel, R. M., and Chacko, Anna W., "Architecture of Distended and Nondistended Human Umbilical Cord." *Contributions to Embryology,* Vol. XXXV, No. 237 (1954).

Shettles, Landrum B., "Further Observations on Living Human Oocytes and Ova." *American Journal of Obstetrics and Gynecology,* Vol. 69, No. 2 (February, 1955).

—, "A Morula Stage of Human Ovum Developed in Vitro." *Fertility and Sterility,* Vol. 6, No. 4 (July–August, 1955).

—, "Observations on Human Follicular and Tubal Ova." *American Journal of Obstetrics and Gynecology,* Vol. 66, No. 2 (August, 1953).

Spaulding, Milo H., "The Development of the External Genitalia in the Human Embryo." *Contributions to Embryology,* Vol. XIII, No. 61 (1921).

Streeter, George L., "Development of the Auricle in the Human Embryo." *Contributions to Embryology,* Vol. XIV, No. 69 (1922).

—, "Developmental Horizons in Human Embryos." *Contributions to Embryology.* Age groups XI, XII: Vol. 30, No. 197 (1942); Age groups XIII, XIV: Vol. 31, No. 199 (1945); Age groups XV, XVI, XVII, XVIII: Vol. 22, No. 211 (1948); Age groups XIX to XXIII (prepared by C. H. Heuser and G. W. Corner): Vol. 34, No. 230 (1951).

—, "Focal Deficiencies in Fetal Tissues." *Contributions to Embryology,* Vol. XXII, No. 126 (November, 1930).

West, Cecil M., "Development of Gums in the Human Fetus." *Contributions to Embryology,* Vol. XVI, No. 79 (1925).

GENERAL ARTICLES

Allen, Robert D., "The Moment of Fertilization." *Scientific American* (July, 1959).

Bronstad, H. V., "The Warning and Promise of Experimental Embryology." *Bulletin of the Atomic Scientist* (March, 1956).

Ebert, James D., "The First Heartbeats." *Scientific American* (March, 1959).

Fischberg, Michael and Blackler, A. W., "How Cells Specialize." *Scientific American* (September, 1961).

Hurwitz, Jerard, and Furth, J. J., "Messenger RNA." *Scientific American* (February, 1962).

Mazia, Daniel, "How Cells Divide." *Scientific American* (September, 1961).

Moscona, A. A., "How Cells Associate." *Scientific American* (September, 1961).

Reynolds, Samuel R. M., "Obstetrical Labor." *Scientific American* (March, 1950).

ABOUT THE AUTHOR

GERALDINE LUX FLANAGAN *was educated at a Vienna* gymnasium *and at Radcliffe College. At the age of nineteen she became a researcher and later a reporter for* Life *Magazine, where she specialized for eight years in news of science and medicine. She is married to Dennis Flanagan, editor of* Scientific American. *She lives with their two children in Princeton, New Jersey. This is her first book.*